Yoking Up

To The

Gospel Plow
To Learn About

Jesus Christ

Yoking Up
To The
Gospel Plow
To Learn About
Jesus Christ

Robert L. Patterson

YOKING UP TO THE GOSPEL PLOW TO LEARN ABOUT JESUS CHRIST

This book is written to provide information and motivation to readers. Its purpose is not to render any type of psychological, legal, or professional advice of any kind. The content is the sole opinion and expression of the author, and not necessarily that of the publisher.

Printed in the United States of America.

ISBN   978-1-64552-111-2   (Hardback)
ISBN   978-1-64552-091-7   (Paperback)
ISBN   978-1-64552-092-4   (Digital)

Lettra Press books may be ordered through booksellers or by contacting:

Lettra Press LLC
18229 E 52nd Ave.
Denver City, CO 80249
1 303 586 1431 | info@lettrapress.com
www.lettrapress.com

Robert L. Patterson

PERSONAL:

Father William Elbert Patterson
Mother Irene Latisha Patterson

Marital Status:
Married to a beautiful woman (Thelma A. Patterson)
4 lovely Children

RELIGIOUS WORKS:

Gospel Preacher and Personal Work Evangelist
Publish a Monthly Tabloid for the Church, and the general Public

PERSONAL AMBITION:

I am just a Nobody trying to tell Everybody about Somebody who can save Everybody, appealing to the lost souls to come to Christ through preaching the gospel behind pulpits, teaching personal in home bible classes, and prayerfully through the reading and teaching of this publication.

My Friends, I am truly thankful to the God of heaven for those of you who have helped and are helping me and my wife to carry out the publishing of the gospel of Christ to as many people in the world as possible.

The Bible said, "The Lord gave the word: great was the company of those that published it" (Psalms 68:11).

Introduction

The object of this book is to share with Preachers, Bible class teachers, and to the General Public information that I have gathered from the Bible, the word of God that will help New Christians in their New Spiritual Walk Of Life, because All New Christians must be fed or nurture as soon as possible so they can grow and gain strength and spiritual understanding so they will become helpful in the kingdom of God, which is the church of Christ.

New Christians must be taught to desire the word of God; similar to a natural born child who have to be taught how to walk or to ride a bicycle, and most of the time they have to be taught more than once.

My prayer to God is that the readers of this book will be enlighten and uplifted in their spirits as they read and use the guidelines that are provided in this book.

The Bible said, "And Jesus said unto him, No Man, Having Put His Hand To The Plough, And Looking Back, Is Fit For The Kingdom Of God" (Luke 9:62).

Robert L. Patterson

Acknowledgements

Acknowledgement is said to be a confession of appreciation and compliment.

First and foremost I want to confess my true appreciation to the God of heaven for giving me the knowledge to read and to understand Christ and the apostles' doctrine, and for the ability to open my mouth and speak boldly as I ought to speak.

I truly want to give a special appreciation to, Diana Sanders, owner of Diana's Creation in Forrest City, Arkansas, for helping and inspiring me to write for many years in her Arkansas Delta Newspaper in Forrest City. I thank her for encouraging me to write my own Gospel of Christ Paper, and for encouraging me to write this book.

I must truly confess that without the wisdom and knowledge of my lovely wife, Thelma Patterson, having her working with me has been fun and very inspirational, she have inspired me greatly and has been a very good colleague. For her; I am most thankful.

I humbly acknowledge my father, Elbert Patterson for his instruction, and my mother, Irene Patterson for her encouraging words of wisdom, to the both of them for loving and teaching me, and the rest of my brothers and sisters not to let what other people say to or about us, cause us to deviate from doing the right things that are in our heart to do.

My deepest gratitude and indebtedness is to you, the readers of this book, I truly hope that it will inspire you in a Godly way. To Preachers, Ministers, Pastors, Clergy's, Teachers, and to all who will use this book as a guide to teach Newly Baptized believers in Christ, how to grow spiritually as they take this great journey into their New Christian Walk of Life.

Contents

The Making Of A Christian

These Are The Things That All People Must Do To Become A Christian:

1. People Must Hear The Word of God: Because it is contained in the scripture that people must be educated by God's word to be saved, according to what John said, in John 6:45, it is contained in the Scriptures, "They shall all be taught of God." Those who learn the truth from him will be connected to his son Jesus Christ.

2. People Must Believe The Word of God: Because without believing the scripture to be the written word of God, then it is absolutely no possible way to be saved, the Hebrew writer was trying to get us to have faith in God when he penned these words in Heb 11:6 without confidence in God's word you will never please him, and without depending on him you will never receive the rewards that he will sincerely give to those who look for him.

3. People Must Repent Of Their Sins: Repentance is to regret the things done in our pass. Paul was trying to motivate the Christians in Corinth to move from their old way, into a new way of life, in 1 Cor 6:11, there was a period in your life when you indulge in all type of wrong doing, just like many others have done, but you are regenerated, set apart for God; and he has accepted you because you turned from your wicked ways.

4. People Must Confess Their Faith in Jesus Christ: Paul said "That if thou shalt confess with thy mouth the Lord Jesus, and shalt believe in thine heart that God hath raised him from the dead, thou shalt be

saved" (Romans 10:9). Making a confession is telling others that you believe that Jesus Christ is the son of God.

5. People Must Be Baptized Into Christ: Baptism is a Spiritual Burial; in order for a person to be spiritually baptized they must be buried in a watery grave of baptism. They cannot simply have water sprinkled or poured on them for baptism. Have you ever seen or heard of a person lying in an open grave and the people sprinkle or pour a little dirt on them and called it a burial? Seriously not, neither is sprinkling or pouring water on a person spiritual baptism in the sight of God. Paul said in order to become a new creature, one have to be submerge in water this is the instruction he gave to the church in Romans 6:4. Your old sinful nature was buried with Christ in baptism when he died; and when God with his glorious power, brought Christ back to life again, you were given that same wonderful New Life to Enjoy.

My Friends, the doctrine on spiritual baptism teaches that the believers were baptized in much water, Please Hear Me; it does not take much water to sprinkle on a person. My Friends, becoming a Christians is a life changing experience that transforms the believers from the Old Carnal Way of Life into a New Spiritual Way of Life in Jesus Christ our Lord.

There are so many people after hearing the gospel of Christ are almost persuaded to become a Christian. My Friends, being almost persuaded is not good enough you must except the word of the gospel and become a Christian to be saved.

The Danger Of Looking Back

Looking back is dangerous because, it can cause Christians to lose focus on the direction in which we were plowing. Looking back is detrimental to one's own soul, because it can cause us to not maintain the peace we have with God, it will stop us from making a good productive crop (harvest) for the Lord. Looking back can cause us to forget the mission that Christ gave us to do, which is to reconcile the world together so when he comes our fruit will receive everlasting Life. Paul said to the church in Philippi to hold on to their faith, and follow the example of other Christians, in Phil 3:15-17, "I hope that you who are mature Christians can see eye-to-eye with me on these things, furthermore if you disagree on some situation, I still believe that God will make it simple for you if you fully obey his word of truth. Beloved brothers, model your lives after mine, and notice who else lives up to my example".

Looking back is dangerous because, when a person is transformed from their old carnal way of life into a new spiritual way of life, that wicked challenger will be there to persuade them to turn back. That is why it is so crucial that the New Members of the body of Christ receive a second teaching by some strong spiritual minded people, who will nourish them with the biblical formula that God prescribed, which is the truthfulness of the word that they will grow. As these New Disciples of Christ continue to grow spiritually they will become fruitful in every work and will be continually increasing in the knowledge of God, strengthened in every capacity according to his glorious power, teaching them that the Lord knows them that are his. Everyone that put on the name of Christ must depart from iniquity. If a person has freed himself from these he shall be a container unto honor, sanctified, assemble for the master's use, *and* prepared unto every good work. Above all, teach them that when they became Christians they took a grip to the Gospel Plow and they should plow in hope and never look back. Luke wrote, "Jesus said to him, Anyone that allow himself to be distracted from the work he plan for them to do is not suitable for the kingdom of God" (Luke 9:62).

Looking back is dangerous because, it can cause us to become unfit for the kingdom of God, the church that Christ promises to construct. Peter demonstrate the behavior of two of the most disgusting events imaginable that will happen to Christians that turn their backs on the Lord. Peter said, "when a person has been forgiven of their wicked ways of this world by learning the good news of our Lord and Savior Jesus Christ, and then get tangled with sin and becomes its slave again, they are worse off than they was before, they would have been better off if they had never learned of him than after learning of him to turn their backs on the holy commandments that were given to them. The old saying is that "A dog comes back to what he has vomited, and a pig is washed only to come back and wallow in the mud again." This is what it is really like when Christians turn again to their sin" (2 Peter 2:20-22).

Looking back is dangerous because, looking back has caused so many people to stumble and fall back into despair and justify themselves and became more unfaithful. Looking back have cause people to start committing all type of uninterrupted sins, they become so blind that they will not even consider returning back to God. Peter made a humble appeal concerning Jesus love for God's people, he said, "The Lord is not idle relating to his pledge, as some men relate to idleness; but is longsuffering for us, and does not want any to be lost, but that all would come and repent" (2 Peter 3:9).

The Great Commission

Teach the New Christians that some of the most misunderstood statements among the religious people of the world today are, when the Lord told his 12 disciples to go into the entire world and preach the gospel to every creature. Today with all of the technology that we have available to receive knowledge through the scriptures, why are there so many gospel preachers who cannot understanding of the 12 disciples of Christ is not told to go into the entire world as we know it today, none of the 12 disciples of Christ visited America, or any other of the five continents, yet they did as Christ command them, they went to the entire world that was in existence during their life time which was Asia.

Teach the New Christians that when Christ was upon the earth he gave his 12 Disciples what is known as the Limited Commission in which they were told absolutely not to go into some particular area.

The Bible said, "These twelve Jesus sent forth, and commanded them, saying, Go not into the way of the Gentiles, and into any city of the Samaritans enter ye not: But go rather to the lost sheep of the house of Israel" (Matthew 10:5-6).

Teach the New Christians that after Christ's resurrection from the grave, he gave his 12 disciples what is known as the Great Commission, which mean that they was commanded to go into the entire world and carry out the commands that he gave them. Now for us to truly understand the Great Commission, we must have some understanding of our world geographically, because it would better help people to understand that the missionary journey of Christ and his 12 disciples did not include the entire 7 continents of the world as we know it today. In the times that the apostles lived on the earth, Asia was the only continent during that time.

Teach the New Christians that the 12 disciples went into their entire world which was scripturally known as Asia, and preached the Gospel to every creature. Furthermore the proof that the 12 disciples completely fulfilled the Great Commission that Christ gave them was on the day of Pentecost, when the Holy Spirit caused all Nations under Heaven to come into one place to hear the word of God.

Teach the New Christians that long after all the 12 disciples died, the world was broken up into what is known today as continents. The people started searching for new land in other parts of the world. In their search they discovered a piece of land and they called it America. After America was discovered, the work to establish the church of Christ in America began on the American frontier during the early 19th Century. During that time Preachers began to teach the doctrine of Christ, teaching people that the church should be called by Christ's name. Now that the church of Christ is established and we are members of it, now we must go and tell the good news unto the whole continent in which we live, and when we do this we are doing exactly what Christ told his Disciples to teach us to do in (Matt 28:19-20).

Teach the New Christians that through the magnificent power of God, the gospel of Christ will go into every continent on this earth. And never forget that Christ did not give the Great Commission to individual to go into the entire 7 different continents to preach the gospel of Christ as some false doctrine gospel preachers would have people to believe.

Personal Work Is An
Individual Responsibility

Teach the New Christians that it is an individual responsibility to work out their own deliverance with fear and reverence, which include the performance of moral and religious acts by which we are personally trying to cause others to hear the Gospel of Christ and be saved. Paul said, "Dear friends, when I was present with you, you were forever so watchful to follow my instructions. And now that I am away you must be even more watchful to do the good things that result from being saved, obeying God with deep reverence, and not shrinking back into all that might displease him" (Phil 2:12).

Teach the New Christians that it is very imperative that they work hard every day and night as if it is the last chance they have to save someone, teach them to believe they are the best rescue people in the world. Rescuing people from the burning condemnation of hell where the souls of so many people will be trapped and lost forever if they do not get the word of God to them while there is still hope. Teach them to always protect themselves from falling from the safety of God's care. Jude said, "Stay focus in the worship of God looking for the forgiveness of our Lord and savior Jesus Christ unto everlasting life. On some having sympathy, making a distinction: some are save with terror, yanking some of *them* out of the fire; hating even the clothing blemished by the flesh. Currently give thanks to him that is able to prevent you from withdrawing, and he will safeguard you and present *you* perfect before the company of his majesty with over and above joyfulness" (Jude 1:21-24).

Teach the New Christians that it is a requirement that Christians should never become lazy in their personal business. They must stay enthusiastic in spirit, stay tolerant in misfortune, always triumphing in optimism, deliver to the need of other Christians, and always give to the unfriendliness of others, because it is our responsibility to be the best personal worker that we can be for the cause of Christ. We should put our best foot forward teaching and baptizing as many people that we can so that their souls will not be lost. Luke said, "A worker came back and gave a report to his superior what those that had been invited said. And his superior became angry and told him to "go swiftly into the Broadway and passageways of the town and invite the hungry, disfigure, crippled, paralyzed, and the unsighted". Yet after all that work, there was still room. So the superior told the worker to "go out into the countryside, and side roads and plead with every one that you meet to come, so that God's house will have a multitude of people" (Luke 14:21-23).

Teach the New Christians that teaching and helping others to become children of God is one of the most greatest and joyful spiritual feelings that Christians can experience. Teach them how to gain the courage and the spiritually powerful to put up with whatsoever things that comes their way. Teach them to stay persuaded, open-minded, and to stay in compliance with his guidelines, so when Christ comes their earthly container can go back to the dust, and their spirit will live with God forever, because they made their calling certain. Matthew said, "the church of Christ began like a little kernel of mustard that someone went and planted it in the ground, in the beginning it was very little, but it grew to become the largest and greatest of all plants, even the birds came and found refuge in it" (Matt 13:31-32). Solomon said, "Godly people grow into a tree that bears living fruit and those that save souls are wise" (Prov 11:30).

Church Goals

Highest quality teaching: My Friends, when we hold the Bible, the word of God in our hands, we have the highest quality teaching book and the power to be saved at our fingertips. If all Christians could understand that when the son of man instructed his handpick group of Disciples to go into every city and hamlet in the entire universe, that he was not giving that command to each individual person to go and teach in each and every district in the universe, rather a universal charge which was to be carry from generation to generation, which is the identical thing that he directed his Disciples to do. Paul said, I am not embarrassed of the word of Christ. Because it is God's powerful process of bringing all that believe it to glory. This letter was delivered first to the Jews only, but in these days everyone is encourage to come to God in the very same way" (Romans 1:16).

The only church that can save souls: The souls of mankind is the most important thing that we have, therefore we should put forth our utmost efforts to save it. The people that work to win souls are wise; the savior of the world came with an aim to find wayward people, which is the exact example that all should be following. Christians should be spending their time trying to bring the wayward back home to the Lord. If those that are trying to mend this religious gap that have spread all over the world would join hands and work together, we can tear down the walls of hatred and racial imbalance, and replace those things with the love of God that is within us. Paul said, "Be gentle and ready to forgive; never hold grudges. Remember, the Lord forgave you, so you must forgive others. Most importantly, let love direct your life, for then the whole house of worship will stay all together in perfect agreement" (Col 3:13-14).

Most spiritual successful: The church of Christ is the most spiritual successful establishment in the world, and for Christians to maintain this triumph they must study and learn the spiritual material that is required by the Creator. One of the most imperative things that the doctrine of Christ teaches is that through it we can gain the inspiration of the almighty, the instruction of his righteousness which will inquire the spiritual mind that will help us to gain the peace of divinity, and to live a good powerful life here on this earth. It is equally important that the new Pilgrims learn to maintain their new spiritual walk for we are as strangers and pilgrims hear on this earth. Paul said, "The complete Bible was approved to us by inspiration from God and is useful to teach us what is true and to make us realize what is wrong in our lives; it straightens us out and helps us do what is right. It is God's way of making us well prepared at every point, fully equipped to do good to everyone" (2 Tim 3:16-17).

Most forgiving: Teach the New Christians we are the most forgiving, because we are taught of God on forgiveness. We are the most forgiving, because we want the Creator to forgive our wrong doing, so then we must forgive those who do wrong against us. Teach the whole group to always continue in the work of the Lord for in the end we shall collect if we do not fall short. And with all the things that you teach the new comers, emphasis to them to toil charitably giving every effort trying to convert some vital souls for the Lord, so when he come again we can enter with him into the eternal home somewhere on the other side. To all preachers and teachers in the churches of Christ you should be making your request to the Creator, asking him to open your understanding so that you can understand his oral speech. Luke said, "Be careful of yourselves, if your brother infringe against thee, reprimand him; and if he be sorry, forgive him" (Luke 17:3).

The Importance Of Worship

—◦⁂◦—

Teach the New Christians the importance of worship services: Worship services are very important, because worship is where people come together to learn of God, and the Lord Jesus Christ. In worship we are taught the ordinances of God that will save us from the fiery condemnation of hell, we are also taught the difference between walking in the light and walking in darkness, in the light is where all of the spiritual blessing are, and in the light all of the faithful Christians have fellowship with one another, worship is where sinners can come and hear the word of God and become Christians, most important of all in worship we are taught how that Christ died for our sins according to the bible, and that he was buried, and on the third day he rose again according to what the bible teach, in worship we are taught never to disregard the congregation gathering together, because some is doing just that and have fallen by the wayside. We are taught to persuade and to inform each other, and do it more often particularly now that Christ coming back is nearer than before.

Teach the New Christians the importance of giving: Giving is one of the most important characteristic in the world; God magnified his love to the world when he gave his only begotten Son, so that mankind would not enter into outer darkness, but will gain everlasting life, through Jesus Christ our Lord. Giving is an observable fact, when a person give from their heart, God will take what they have giving and will multiply it and give it back to the giver again. Christians that are sincere hearted will give unconditionally regardless of their own personal circumstances. There is another fact concerning giving, that is new Christians must be taught to give themselves to the Lord, and to the preached word of the gospel.

Teach the New Christians to dress modestly: Teach the young women to pattern themselves after the manner of the holy women in the old times that trusted in God's word, and who did not get carried away with any amazement. Teach them that it is nothing wrong with them being a righteous person, for a righteous woman is worth more than any amount of money. Teach them not to fashion themselves after the women of the world, but to be self-effacing. Teach the unmarried women to remain faithful to the Lord, and to be holy in their body and in spirit which is the Lord's. Teach both the females and males to dress in a manner that is appealing to the working class of people and the Lord. Teach them to study so they will be accepted by God, and do not be embarrassed while working truly hard explaining the word of God to others.

Teach the New Christians to fellowship with one another: Teach the new Christians that fellowship is of great importance, because in fellowship two are better than one, for if one fall the other one will help him up, also two working together can get more done than one. Teach the new Christians to remain unwavering in the apostles' teaching. Fellowship teaches us acts of kindness, eating bread, and praying from each other homes, fellowship give Christians a true happiness in a universal bond, and gives the family of God an opportunity to get to know one another, it also offered a great opportunity to save some lost souls. The Bible said, "Admiring God and the entire town was approving of them, and each day God was adding to the church those who were being saved" (Acts 2:47).

My friends, it is extremely important to teach New Christians that whenever there is a problem fixed the problem and not the blame, teach them that there will always be people going against them regardless to how good they behave themselves because wrongdoings will come, but the resolve and the blessings is in the ones that take the wrong. Christ said, "Woe unto the world because of offences! for it must needs be that offences come; but woe to that man by whom the offence cometh! Wherefore if thy hand or thy foot offend thee, cut them off, and cast them from thee: it is better for thee to enter into life halt or maimed, rather than having two hands or two feet to be cast into everlasting fire" (Matthew 18:7-8). Paul said, "Recompense to no man evil for evil. Provide things honest in the sight of all men. If it be possible, as much as lieth in you, live peaceably with all men. Dearly beloved, avenge not yourselves, but rather give place unto wrath: for it is written, Vengeance is mine; I will repay, said the Lord" (Romans 12:17-19).

Serving God Without Distractions

One of the most difficult things to get New Christians to understand is that the word of God teaches all Christians that we absolutely cannot love sinful things, nor participate in the worldly activities that are taking place in the world without totally going against the word of God. Those who are older Christians must teach the New Christians by teaching them the word of God, and by setting good spiritual examples for them to follow. Teach the new Christians the importance of knowledge, wisdom and understanding, teach them the bare essentials ground rules of the church so that the newly baptized Christians can grow up and serve in Christ's Kingdom without any distractions. Teach the New Christians now that their hearts are pure they can see everything that is pure. Furthermore we must teach the New Christians how to grow from a spiritual childhood into a spiritual mature person. John said, "Stop getting involved with and loving the things of this evil world and all that it promise you, for when you adore those things you show that you do not actually love God; for all these worldly things, these evil needs, the craving for sex, the desire to acquire everything that is appealing to you, and the pleasure that comes from riches surely these thing are not from God. They are from this demonic evil world only" (1 John 2:15-16).

Serve God without confusion, the God of heaven is not the creator of confusion, but of harmony, as in every congregation of the saints. Where jealousy and conflict *is*, there *is* confusion and all kind of evil arguments. The knowledge that comes from heaven is first clean, peaceful, pleasant; willing to give in to others, full of pity and good fruits, without prejudice, and without double standards. It was planted in righteousness and in harmony in those that make harmony. Let our enemy be dressed in disgrace and humiliation, and allow them to be cover up in their own confusion. God is with us as a powerful dreadful one: therefore our persecutors will trip and fall and they shall not overcome: they shall be very much ashamed; for they shall not do well: their eternal confusion shall never be over. Paul said, "The God of heaven is not one who likes things to be unmanageable and unruly. He wants thing to be in harmony, and he looks for the same things in all of the churches of Christ" (1 Cor 14:33).

Teach the New Christians to serve God without leisure activity interfering, such as festivals, public holidays, local holidays, celebration days, anniversary days, feast days, saint's days, or any other so-called Holy Day. To all Christians warriors of Christ do not allow yourselves to become tied up in the worthless affairs of this life, for in doing so you cannot make the one happy who signed you up in his military. No man that goes to war tangled himself up with the affairs of this life; so that he will be able to give pleasure to the one who hath selected him to be a warrior. My Friends, the weapons that we fight with are not worldly, but spiritual and we must fight this war through the power of God's word, because we are not warring against human being, we are warring against the ruler of darkness, the prince of the devil. Paul said, "We are not fighting against human being, but against spirits without bodies those evil rulers of the invisible world, those mighty satanic beings and great evil princes of darkness who rule this world; and against huge numbers of wicked spirits in the spirit world. So the Christians warrior must use every piece of God's protective covering to resist the enemy whenever he attacks, and when it is all over, you will still be standing up" (Eph 6:12-13). Paul said, "furthermore if you are trying to gain sympathy from God by what you do on specified days of the months and years, so that you cannot serve him it will not matter at all with God" (Gal 4:10).

Giving Will Bring Blessings From God

Teach the New Christians there is something special about God concerning giving that mankind may never fully understand, but one thing is certain, is that the more people give to God the more God gives to people, therefore God will greatly bless those who will give according to what he have giving unto them, because God love those who give with a pleasant disposition. He will also bring about some terrible things to those who will steal from him, and those who keep back part of the things that he has giving to them. Teach the new Christians and the entire congregation to stay right with God in their giving for our time can expire at any moment upon this earth. Teach the church that in order for us to receive the ultimate blessings that God will give, we have to exceed the religious things that the denominational people are doing. Luke said, "For whosoever of you will give, you will receive, your contribution will come back to you jam-packed and in abundant quantity, hard-pressed, suppressed together so that you can receive more, in overflowing quantity, because in the same quantity that you give big or little, it will be the same one that will be use to give the right quantity to you again" (Luke 6:38).

Teach the New Christians that there will be difficult days ahead on this Christian journey, therefore teach them to make being Christians the first priority in their lives. Teach them that regardless of the task that God may give them to do, do it with a willing mind, for that is accepted with God. Teach them to never allow the devil to temp them into becoming greedy with the possessions that God have given them to enjoy, and always share them with others. Paul said, "the churches of Christ in the town of Macedonia, went beyond the apostles greatest expectation, the initial thing that those Christians did was to commit themselves to the Lord and to the apostles, waiting for whatsoever guidelines that God might give to them through the teaching of the apostles" (2 Cor 8:5).

Teach the New Christians when they are down in what appears to be a horrifying condition, and it look as if they are standing in quick sand, don't worry, just wait unwearyingly on the Lord, for truly he will pay attention to those that are calling out to him. He will bring them out, and guide them in the right direction. The Almighty God of our fathers, who shall help us, and shall bless us with the blessings of heaven above if we be found faithful. David said, "Wait unwearyingly on God to help you, because he pays attention to the prayers from an honest and sincere heart. He will pick you up out of the ditch of misery, out of the overwhelming filthy conditions of life, and will set your feet on a solid foundation, and will secure you as you go onward. He will give you a new cry to chant, to pay tribute to our God. A lot of people will hear of the wonderful things he did for you, and will stand in amazement looking unto the Lord, and will put their hope in him. Numerous blessings will be given to those who will put their confidence in the Lord and have no faith in those who are arrogant or who trust in manmade religions" (Psalms 40:1-4).

Teach all Christians the greatest gifts that we can give to God is to have obeyed his word. The judgment is coming and will be very dreadful; there will be nothing to look forward to for those who have not obeyed the word of God. But the terrible punishment of God's awful anger, Paul said, "To you who are concerned relax with us, when the Lord Jesus shall be made known from heaven with his powerful angels, In blazing fire taking revenge on those who do not know God, and have not obeyed the gospel of the Lord Jesus Christ" (2 Thess 1:7-8).

Meditate On The Word Of God

All New Christians should be taught the characteristic of meditating as soon as possible, for it is a powerful link in inquiring a healthy well-balanced spiritual life. Christians should find a place of solitude where they can consider or reflect at length on ways of clearing their mind from all the cares and problems that bombard and clutters their lives. Teach the New Christians to read the scripture and consider them carefully at length, meditating day and night thinking them over in their mind so that they can retain the things that they have studied; as a result they will grow spiritually and be able to teach others also. Paul said, "You know how, when you were a little boy, you were taught the Holy Scriptures, by your mother's mother Lois, and your mother Eunice, it is these scriptures that will make you wise to believe God's deliverance by your trust in Jesus Christ. The whole Bible was given to us by the will of God and is useful to teach us what is true and to make us realize what is wrong in our lives; it makes our lives straight and helps us do what is right" (2 Tim 3:15-16).

Teach the New Christians, that meditating on spiritual matters is exactly what it will take to replenish our minds, and to do this Christians have to reestablish their priority in life. My Friends, when Jesus Christ was baptized he went away from the people that he had been associating with, and went into a place of privacy and engaged himself in a devotional exercise that was to lead him for the rest of his life. Luke said, "Soon after Jesus was baptized, being full with the Holy Spirit, went from Jordan River, and was directed by the spirit of God to go out into the desolate desert land of Judea, where the Devil enticed him for forty days. Jesus had not eating anything all that time and was extremely famished. The Devil said unto him, if you are truly the son of God, then make this stone to become a cake of bread, but Jesus said, it is contained in the

Scriptures that there or things, in life much more important than bread only. My friends, when Jesus Christ was meditating out in the desert after his baptism, he was contemplating a plan in his mind on what he was intending to do concerning the situation that the Devil was going to try to entice him into doing" (Luke 4:1-4).

Teach the New Christians that meditation is a devotional exercise of the mind and through studying and meditating on the scriptures it will lead them in the right alleyway. It will give light to their canyon when they are dark and dreadful, it will make them to trump in the company of their adversary, and it will replace all of the things that can cause their spirit to be bewildered. It also will help serve as a beckoning light to signal the wayward travelers so they can see their spiritual light shining in them so they can find their way home to the shepherd of our soul who would not have one sheep to be lost. Meditating is what describe to us and make us to recognize and distinguish the spiritual from the carnal; the unclean from the clean, a distention that must be understood in order to worship and serve God exclusively, for the scripture say that a person cannot serve God in the flesh. Paul said, "Pursuing after the Holy Spirit of God will lead to life and peace, but pursuing after your old flesh leads to destruction because the old sinful flesh that we have is against God. It never has obeyed God's commandments and it never will. That is why those who are still under the control of their old sinful flesh, bent on following their old evil fleshly desires, can never please God. But you are not like that, you are controlled by your new spiritual nature if you have the Spirit of God living in you. Remember that if anyone that doesn't have the Spirit of Christ living in them, they are not a Christian at all" (Romans 8:6-9).

Learning How To Pray

Teach the New Christians that Christians do not know how to pray of their own intelligent, mankind pray for things of the flesh. We do not know what to pray for as we really should, therefore we need the help of the Holy Spirit to go between us and God, explaining to God the things that are on our hearts that we are trying to say in our prayers to God, and as human beings, therefore we need some spiritual help. Paul said, "It is because of our faith that the Holy Spirit helps us with our day to day problems and in our praying. For we don't know what we should even be praying for nor how to pray for it as we ought to, but the Holy Spirit talks to God for us with such emotion that it cannot be expressed in words" (Romans 8:26).

Teach the New Christians that prayer is the only way that Christians can communicate with God, and in order to do that, a person have to be righteous and Godly, because God watches for those who have obeyed his word and he listen when they talk to him. He have turned his back on those that refuse to obey him, even though man will not obey God's word he still through his good nature waits patiently on the evil, the heinous, and those who continue to have an unrighteous way of thinking to come to him so he will forgive them of their wrongdoing. He is unwilling that anyone should miss out on having an everlasting life. John said, "God loved this world in so great extent that he gave up his only Son so that everybody who believes on him would not be lost but have everlasting life. "For God did not send Christ into this world to destroy it, but to save and deliver his people from their sin" (John 3:16-17).

Teach the New Christians that God has a sympathetic relationship between him and the personal affairs of his people. Teach all Christians in order to gain this relationship with God, the people of God has to be transform from the old carnal way of life, into the new spiritual way of life so they can come before his throne of grace in love and humble adoration recognizing him as the Father which is in heaven, honoring his name in the highest. David said, "Generate dear Lord in me a new, clean spirit, O Lord, filled me with overflowing clean ways of thinking, and give me a right heart. Do not throw me away, nor expel me forever from your company. Do not take the Holy Spirit from me" (Psalms 51:10-11).

Teach the New Christians to pray that the love of all saints may succeed, especially in this troublesome multitude of unbelieving sinners and unfaithful backsliding Christians who have turn this world spiritually upside down. In today's world we need the prayers of the righteous to cry out to God in an unyielding sincere way. Teach the new Christians while they are praying if they bear in mind that somebody have sin or done wrong against them, instruct them that they must forgive those who have done them wrong, because if they do not forgive them, then neither will God forgive them when they sin or do wrong to others. Teach the new Christians that the power of prayer has stopped people from dying it has added years to people lives. Prayer and faith has been known to heal the broken hearted and to set people free from prison walls. My Friends, I am completely persuaded that Jesus Christ is coming back after his Kingdom, his church. So my prayer is that you all will obey the gospel of Jesus Christ, and become Christians before the end come. Paul said, "When Christ comes back, all the people who died in him will become alive again. After that the end will come when he have transported his church back to heaven, and then he will turn over all of his authority of the Kingdom to God the Father, who have put all enemies under Christ feet" (1 Cor 15:23-24).

Loving People From The Bible Point Of View

My friends, Love is the most powerful thing in the cosmos and human beings who have been fortune enough to contain it have the power to do unimaginable things. Love can make people laugh, cry, and dance for joy, love will make you feel happy without you understanding why, out of all the things that love can and will do, love does not make you hate anyone, whatsoever they do. Peter gave warning to all those who harness themselves to the love of God.

Peter said, "But the end of all things is at hand: be ye therefore sober, and watch unto prayer.

Most important of all things have earnest love among yourselves: for love shall cover the multitude of sins" (1 Peter 4:7-8).

My friends, if all gospel preachers, religious leaders, parents, and guardians would encourage the people that they are in charge of, to investigate the Scriptures on a daily basis, then perhaps we could get the people to understand what Paul was conveying in Acts 17 that when a person read the Scriptures for themselves, they will get a personal understanding of the word of God that will stay with them.

Paul said, "These were more noble than those in Thessalonica, in that they received the word with all readiness of mind, and searched the scriptures daily, whether those things were so" (Acts 17:11).

My friends, the greatest Love of all mankind is the love that Jesus Christ demonstrated for the world when he gave his life on that old rugged cross on Calvary Hill in Jerusalem, where he was humiliated between two male criminals, and even there, in that most dreadful condition, Christ gave one of those criminal complete pardoned according to his word.

The Bible said, "And when they were come to the place, which is called Calvary, there they crucified him, and the malefactors, one on the right hand, and the other on the left. Then said Jesus, Father, forgive them; for they know not what they do. And they parted his raiment, and cast lots. And he said unto Jesus, Lord, remember me when thou comest into thy kingdom. And Jesus said unto him, Verily I say unto thee, To day shalt thou be with me in paradise" (Luke 23:33-34, 42-43).

My friends, one of the greatest love stories in the Bible concerning friends, is where two men met for the first time and they was joined together by their souls because of love, these two men were best friends instantaneously and they loved each other from then on, they loved each other so much that one of them went against his father in order to protect his friend from the hatred of his father,

Samuel said, "When King Saul had finished talking to David, the spirit of Jonathan was interwoven with the spirit of David, and Jonathan loved David as his own spirit. And David's father took Jonathan that very day, and wouldn't let him return to his father's home any more. Then Jonathan and David vowed a vow, because they loved each other as it was their own spirit" (1 Sam 18:1-3).

My friends, one of the most powerful and astounding relationship in the Bible is where two women, a mother-in-law and her daughter-in-law, who live in the same town became widows. The mother-in-law decided to leave and go back to her blood family in a different land, so she told her daughter-in-law of her intensions. The daughter-in-law loved her mother-in-law with all of her heart, she made her mother-in-law a promise that if she would allow her to go with her, that she would make her mother-in-law's God to become her God, where she lived, she would live also, and where she died, she would die also. Only if her mother-in-law would allow it. This powerful love story proves that death should be the only thing that can separate friends who have been knitted together with the power of God's love.

The Bible said, "And Ruth said, Intreat me not to leave thee, or to return from following after thee: for whither thou goes, I will go; and where thou lodges, I will lodge: thy people shall be my people, and thy God my God: Where thou die, will I die, and there will I be buried: the Lord do so to me, and more also, if ought but death part thee and me. When she saw that she was satisfied minded to go with her, then she left speaking unto her" (Ruth 1:16-18).

John said, "Love is demonstrated when a person gives up their life for the life of their friends" (John 15:13).

Solomon said, "A friend loves at all times, and a brother is born for adversity" (Proverbs 17:17).

Furthermore Solomon said, "A man that hath friends must shew himself friendly: and there is a friend that stickiest closer than a brother" (Proverbs 18:24).

My friends, now you can truly see why people who want to have friends must present themselves friendly, friends who have harness the power of God's love will remain close to each other through all kind of difficulties and misfortunes. A friendship that is perfectly unity as one have acquired the most charming, attractive, and fragrance characteristics of love, it will always nurture and facilitate a lifetime of happiness.

Wisdom, Understanding, And Knowledge

Wisdom is the most important thing in the world; it was created absolutely by God. It is the standard of an honest and praiseworthy way of life to all creations that have or will walk upon this earth. God will give his Holy Spirit of wisdom only to the intelligent minded people; because irrational minded people look down on wisdom, they play religious games and those that watch as they pass by observed their disobedience and disorderly behavior that they play in the sight of man and God. When a person have received the spirit of wisdom, they can comprehend the enticement the devil have stored in the spirit of darkness, but they that have the spirit of wisdom will rejoice in knowing that the greatest spirit of all is the spirit of wisdom, which will not allow them to be entangled with the affairs that the devil have to offer them, but will receive a spirit that will help them to break away from his cunning strategy. Solomon said, "Truly wisdom is the most important thing, therefore all mankind should get wisdom, and of all the things that they have acquired, be sure to acquired understanding" (Prov 4:7).

Understanding is bringing together the exact information that is acquired through practice or revealed in learning. There is a Carnal understanding, and a Spiritual understanding. In this study we want to focus on the Spiritual understanding. One of the major characteristic of understanding is that one must have the ability to figure out what is being said. Spiritual minded people have been transformed from the old carnal fleshly way of understanding, into a new spiritual way of life, a transformation that takes place in a person life when they become a Christian, because it is in baptism where people die, and are reborn, it is where God destroyed the old carnal, sinful mind, he replaced it with a new spiritual mind. Spiritual minded people must be taught the word of God, in order to understand and to comprehend what the will of God is.

Paul said, "When the congregations come together to worship, I rather speak in words that people can understand and be helped by them than by some unidentified language. Beloved brethren, do not be childlike in your understanding of God word. Remain blameless as little children when it comes to arranging to do evil, nevertheless be men in your capabilities and understanding all type of problems" (1 Cor 14:19-20).

Spiritual knowledge is the grouping of truthful information that one has learned and stored in their mind, it includes facts, ideas, and the totality of the truth. The spirit of God will open a person spiritual understanding, allowing them to hear, believe, and retain in their knowledge the good news of the gospel of Christ. Furthermore those Christians who refuse the spiritual knowledge of God, he will command the Holy Spirit to annihilate them, simply because they refuse to learn the knowledge of God after he has given them the opportunity to do so. Some people can hear the word and have complete knowledge of what is being said to the utmost, and still they will reject it and turn a death ear to the word of God. The same thing many people do when they hear the good news of the gospel. John said, "All those who refuse to obey Christ's word, will be judged by the truth that he have spoken in the Day of Judgment. Christ was not speaking of his own thoughts, nevertheless he was told by God the Father what to tell the world. And Christ was sure that the instructions that he had received would lead people to an everlasting life; therefore whatsoever God told Christ he truthfully told it to the world. My Friends, refusing the knowledge of God, is like refusing to go through an open door that will lead you to heaven, and then use all of your energy to knock down and go through a door that you are positively sure that it will lead you to hell" (John 12:48-50).

The Righteous People Of God

Teach the New Christians that the righteous is a group of people who have been called out of the world by obeying the word of God, and has been translated into the kingdom of his dear son, Jesus Christ. And those that are in Christ must build a strong conviction on the things that they are taught by the word of God. Those who are baptized into Christ are called Christians, a promise that God made to his people by the prophets. The word of God teaches that the initial thing that New Christians must understand is that they are in the kingdom of God, and they must learn his way of righteousness. There are many people that are misinformed concerning the righteousness of God, and are trying to setup their own way of being righteous, totally disregarding the righteousness of God. If the world is going to be saved, it will be saved through the righteousness of God which is in Christ Jesus our Lord. Paul said, "When a person becomes a Christian, they becomes a new person spiritually. They are not the same anymore, a new spiritual life has begun! These new things are from the righteousness of God who brought us back to himself through Jesus Christ. God has given us the opportunity to influence everybody to come into his goodwill and be reunited to him. For God was in Christ, reinstating the people of the world back to himself in righteousness, no longer rolling their sins ahead of them, but permanently forgiving them" (2 Cor 5:17-19). This is the wonderful work that Jesus Christ has given for all of us to do.

Teach the New Christians that the righteous husbands must love, encourage, and appreciate his Christian family, in the same way that Christ love and care for the church, therefore he must spend quality time in studying the bible and learning of Christ, so that he can imitate and pass it on to his family, making sure that he will not have to worry about any type of imperfections to come in and destroy them. The righteous husbands will make known to his friends, and fellow citizen that regardless to whose righteousness they choose to go after, that him and his family was most certainly going to worship and follow the Lord. Furthermore the righteous know that the righteousness of men will only lead to everlasting condemnation, because only the righteousness of God will lead the faithful Christians to life everlasting. Peter said, "The souls of people who, long before live in Noah days, they refused to listen to God, even though he remain long suffering for them while Noah was building the ark. However it was only a few people that were saved from drowning in the flood. in which way baptism is a demonstration that we are saved by water through the resurrection of Jesus Christ, baptism does not wash our bodies clean, rather it cleanse our hearts and renew our spiritual relationship with God. And now Christ is in heaven, sitting in the place of honor next to God the Father, and with all the powers that be, even the angels are bowing before him and obeying him" (1 Peter 3:20-22).

Teach the New Christians that as long as Christians stay righteous, God will never forsake them nor leave them helpless, he will always be there for them, even though time after time we have to warn them. Ezekiel said, "When a righteous man turn from his righteousness, and commit wickedness, God will lay some obstruction before him, and he shall die: for the reason that you did not warn him, he shall die in his wrongdoing, and his righteousness which he hath done shall not be remembered; but his wrongdoing you will have to answer for. Nevertheless if you warn the righteous man, that the righteous stop his wrongdoing, and he stop sinning, he shall surely live, because he has been inform; also you hast saved your soul from condemnation" (Ezek 3:20-21).

The Importance Of Keeping
The Lord's Day Holy

Sunday should be set apart specifically for solemn assembling, and religious purposes only; because it is contain in the Old Testament scriptures that the people was instructed not to do any personal activity for the satisfaction of men on the Sabbath Day. Furthermore the very night that Jesus was handed over to the crowd of sinners, he inaugurated communion, established the New Testament, gave his flesh to eat for the life of the world, and his blood to drink for the removing of their sins, showing the world that those who eat his flesh, and drink his blood in a spiritual manner he will live in them, and they in him. Therefore all gospel preachers and religious leaders should be teaching that the Lord's Day in the New Testament have the same significant as the Sabbath Day had in the Old Testament. Accordingly we should respect and keep the Lord's Day Holy in the New Testament time in the same regard as they respected the Sabbath day in the Old Testament time. The Bible said, "Christ inquired from his disciples, asking them did they believe who he was. Simon Peter responded by saying, you are Christ, God's Son. Then God blessed Simon, Jesus said for my heavenly Father has personally exposed this to you this is not from any humankind. Christ said you are Peter, and upon this rock hard solid infallible truth I will construct my church; and all the powers of hell shall not overcome it" (Matt 16:15-18). Furthermore My friends, isn't it ludicrous that almost any grown person will tell you they believe that Christ gave his life for his church, and the New Testament, yet will not believe that the church is the church of Christ, and they confess to be Christian, Christ like.

Teach the New Christians that Sunday is a Holy Day, a day of worship and should be look upon by all spiritual minded Christians in the

29

same manner as the Holy Bible command us to. Bible believing people believe that whatsoever is writing in the Old Testament is there so that the people in the New Testament will have some sound proof that there is something greater to look forward to than just living and dying in our sin. And furthermore we learn that God will provide endurance, control, and support to help us to live in absolute agreement with one another, which is the same behavior that we will learn from Christ in the New Testament. If all Christian's brothers and sisters would understand the fundamental of being a family, the pleasantness of being in perfect harmony, therefore we would have others to help when times are difficult. John said, "Christ gave his disciples a new commandment telling them to love each other in the same large amount as he loves them. Their powerful love for each other will confirm to the entire world that they are his disciples" (John 13:34-35).

My friends, in the Old Testament, the people on the Sabbath Day came and did their sacrifice unto God in the morning, and evening, furthermore in all honesty and truth we the New Testament Christians should be worshipping and praying Devine homage to God in the highest respect that is required for us to do on the Lord's Day in the morning worship service, and in the evening worship service without fail. On the Day of Pentecost when the disciples was gathered together in the temple, people was saying that the disciples were drunk, then Peter told them it is too early in the morning for people to be drunk, because it was only about 9:00 A.M., Acts 2:15. Also Peter went to the Temple one afternoon with John to take part in the 3:00 P.M. evening prayer meeting, Acts 3:1. On one Lord's Day, Paul taught unto midnight planning to leave the next day, Acts 20:7.

The So-Called Five Avenues Of Worship

People assemble themselves together to worship God enthusiastically, with regard, adoration, loyalty, reverent love, and to be in agreement with God. Worship is where people come to pray and performs other religious obligation to express their homage to God, Jesus Christ, and the Holy Spirit. Worship is a God given privilege that he have giving to all mankind without cost, and yet there are some people in the church of Christ saying that Christians cannot come before the throne of God and worship him without doing what they call the five avenues of worship, which include Preaching, Praying, Singing, taking Communion, and Giving money. They say that people cannot worship God acceptably without doing these five things in combination. These men are absolutely preposterous, misleading, and are totally disregarding the doctrine of Christ by their lack of knowledge of the word of God, and are causing those that are following then to be in danger of hell fire, and everlasting destruction, the very thing that people go to worship to save themselves from. David said, "Perform your work to the Lord with happiness, approach his present singing. Keep in your mine that the Lord is God, and he made mankind, they did not make themselves, we are the people of God, and the sheep of his field. Go into his entrance with blessing, and into his magistrates praising, live grateful before him, bless his name forever. The Lord is excellent, his compassion is forever, and his information will last through every age group" (Psalms 101:2-5).

Teach the New Christians that Preaching, Praying, Singing, taking Communion, and Giving money, all these things are of the utmost important in the sight of God, according to the scripture. However, to say that a person cannot worship and praise God without giving money is absolutely erroneous, because there are so many scriptures that teach where people came and worship God having no money.

Furthermore the scriptures tell us that if we come before God and our mind is excited, then God will accept what a person has, not what he do not have. Therefore if a person is excited to give to God whatsoever they have, God will give to them a blessing from heaven. My Friends, we worship before the almighty God of Heaven, the God that will give his children food, water, and clothing without currency. Christians should demonstrate their understanding in worship, in humbleness, disregarding their own selves neither in honor nor in the pleasing of the flesh. Furthermore Christians that worship the true and living God, the God that delivered the Jewish nation and now have given deliverance to all that correctly worship God the Father and the Holy Spirit in the truth. John said, "He said to me, observe but don't do anything like that. I also perform services of Jesus Christ the same as you are, like the brothers and the prophets are doing, the same as all the people who paid attention to the truth confirmed in this book worship God abandoned" (Rev 22:9).

My Friends, teach the New Christians, and all mankind that the only thing that God require to worship him is to "worship him in Spirit and in Truth". My Friends, sometime we as Christians may find ourselves walking down the pathway of destruction, but God's love and mercy, will keep us from the terror of the wicked one, therefore we should look for the pathway that will lead us back to the house of God, and when we get there we should remain in it forever. Paul said, "When I first started preaching the gospel no man stood with me, other than the Lord remained with me and presented to me the chance to courageously preach a complete sermon for the entire world to pay attention to. Plus he saved me from being destroyed by the Flesh eating creatures" (2 Tim 4:16-17).

There Is Only One Church

Teach the New Christians, that the scriptures teach infallibly and methodically that there is only one church found in the entire Bible. Therefore these religious denominations that man has constructed and they call them churches is no more than another misleading idea of the devil. When Christ constructed his spiritual house, he called it his church, it is a place where all mankind can come to hear the word of God, be forgiven of their sins, receive salvation, and those who live and die faithfully will gain everlasting Life. Therefore, when the Devil realized that Christ had constructed a spiritual church, he came up with the idea to persuade preachers to construct him a synagogue, a carnal building and called it church, to mislead people and keep them in darkness while believing that they are saved by being members in a denominational church of their choice, which is nothing but the synagogue of the Devil. Furthermore the Devil knew that if he could convince mankind to believe that all churches belong to Christ, by doing this he would have them accusing Christ of committing spiritual adultery which he knew was a sin for the people to do. Mankind knew through the word of God that the Devil came with the intent to slaughter, imprison, and to annihilate all that live in this world of darkness, and those that are members of the church of Christ. Paul said, "Unreachable distance above any other sovereign or kings or every person in charge. His name is to be far more glorious than that of anyone else either in this world or in the world to come. And the God of heaven has put all things under Christ's feet and placed him as the utmost Head of the church. It is his church, entirety full up in himself, and God gave everything everywhere unto him" (Eph 1:21-23).

My Friends, there are many biblical characteristic that distinctly prove the authenticity of the church of Christ. Daniel, one of the Old

Testament Prophets made it crystal clear when he foretold with sureness that God was going to construct a celestial kingdom in the earth in admiration of his son, Jesus Christ. He penned these words, "And in the years of these kings shall the God of heaven construct a kingdom, which will not be damaged: and the kingdom shall not be given over to mankind, but it will split into pieces and devour all these earthly kingdoms, and it shall remain standing forever" (Dan 2:44). Jesus Christ the son of God made it thoroughly obvious when he made this profound statement "and upon this rock I will build my church; and I will give unto thee the keys of the kingdom of heaven" (Matt 16:18-19). Mark, one of Christ's disciples said "that people will be living on the earth and will see the kingdom of God come with power" (Mark 9:1). The Prophesy of Daniel, the preaching of Christ and his disciples came into existence on the day of Pentecost, Acts 2:1-5.

Another characteristic that distinctly prove the authenticity of the church of Christ, is the foundation in which the church of Christ is built upon. My Friends, before they built the Sears building in Chicago, Illinois after the necessary preparation was made, they laid the foundation and began to build, and after the building was completed, that beautiful sky scraper with all of these lovely rooms inside, the foundation was called the Sears Building. Please hear me, the church that Christ built, he is the foundation, and it does not matter how many churches is build upon it they all should be called by the name of the foundation on which it stand, The church of Christ. For Paul distinctly said, "I have laid the foundation, and there is no additional foundation that can be laid other than Jesus Christ" (1 Cor 3:10-11). Furthermore it does not matter what the denominational people say, the foundation that Christ laid will stand forever, and Christ know those who are members of his church"

Who Called Men To Preach?

Who called man to preach the gospel of Christ, God or man? This question has baffled mankind for many years mainly because they cannot correctly separate the Holy Scriptures relating to Preachers of the gospel of Christ. There was a man called Saul, who was a malicious person that was deliberately harmful to God's people, one day as Saul was journeying to a particular city, Christ appeared unto him, and informed him to go into that city and talk to a man that God have waiting for him. After Saul met and talked with the man name Ananias, he was baptized. Before Saul became a Christian, he was educated by a man call "Gamaliel", and because of the misunderstanding concerning the teaching of "Gamaliel", it has lead people to believe that before a man can become a preacher of the gospel of Christ they must attend some school of religion, and be taught by some man. Please hear me, "Gamaliel" taught Saul the law of their fathers, not the gospel of Christ, as some would have you to believe. Furthermore it is absolutely Ludicrous, for someone to believe that a person, who is not a Christian, can teach and convert another none Christian, and then ordain them to preach the gospel of Christ. When God called Saul to preach his word Saul answer the call and did not receive any teaching or instructions from other men. God only, not "Gamaliel" nor any other man can call men to preach the word of God. He gives them wisdom to use their ability in the fullest. The men that God call can preach his word without receiving the permission from any man. Preachers must not turn away from nor be ashamed of the things that they must preach from the Holy Scriptures.

My Friends, here are some characteristic of the preachers that God called. They can cause people to completely grow in a spiritual way, Col 1:9. They can cause people to differentiate between things that are Godly and things that are not Godly, Ezek 44:23. They can cause people to believe in the word so much that they can move any obstacles that stand in their pathway, Matt 21:21. They can cause people to hear, believe, repent, confess, and be baptized for the remission of their sins, Acts 2:38. They can give people the right to partition the almighty God of heaven in prayer, 1 Peter 3:12. They can cause people to believe that they can do anything that are humanly possible through the word of God, Phil 4:13. They can cause people to conquer their greatest fears, 2 Tim 1:7. They can cause people to believe that it does not matter what type of physical, emotional, or spiritual condition the devil have trap them in, God have provided a way out of all those horrendous things, 1 Cor 10:13. They can cause people to hold on to God when it looks as if all hope is gone, friends or gone, abandon by the family, maybe your health is deteriorating, and you believe that you are sinking beneath the misery of it all, yet there is a small voice in your mind saying hang in there and make another request, and wait on the Lord, Psalms 40:1-2.

Here are some characteristic of some preachers that God did not call: The preachers that teach lies, false visions, unfaithful words, and that lie on God, Jer 23:28-32. Preachers that affirm, that they are an apostle of Christ, 1 Cor 15:8-9.

Truly, there are no apostles in the world today, and if there are, they are artificial apostles, deceivers working undercover for the devil, 2 Cor 11:12-14. And there are some artificial preachers that are being called "Reverend" which is one of the names that the God of heaven was called, Psalms 111:9.

Contents

F Y I

Have You Added This Characteristic To Your Faith?

Do you display the characteristic of your confident in the truth? Do you have the knowledge of the truth so that you can maintain in conflict? Are you faithful? Are you eloquent and mighty in the scripture? Do you take a firm confidential stand against all of the spiritual wickedness that you encounter day by day? Do you always stand in a very presumptuous manner knowing that your confidence is built on nothing less that the precious blood of God's dear Son Jesus Christ who died for all mankind? And gave us the confidence of eternal life to those who do the truth? "Christ as a son over his own kingdom; in whose kingdom are we, if we cleave to the self-assurance and the triumph of the trust solid unto the last day" (Heb 3:6).

Do you display the characteristic of your labor of love? In your labor of love are you just telling people that you love them, or are you proving to them that you love them by the things you are doing for them from your sincere spirit? Do you treat your fellow citizen and your Christian brothers as well as you treat yourself? John said, "Christians, let us quit just saying we love mankind; let us actually love them, and prove it by our manner. Then all will know for sure, by our manner, that we are on God's side, and our spiritual mind will be clear, even when we appear before the Lord" (1 John 3:18-19).

Do you display the characteristic of your endurance? When you have made a request to God for something and you are expecting the fulfillment of it and it seems as if your request has not been heard and what you was looking forward to have been denied? Anyone that has the courage can remove any obstacle that stands in their way, and if they will not be slow to act in their heart for if they think carefully about those things which they have said, it will come to be theirs; Therefore whatsoever things that a person request from God, they must believe that they will be delivered to them, Mark 11:23-24.

Do you display the characteristic of a Christian soldier? by wearing all of your protective covering, and are you positioning yourself so that you can stand and fight against the deceitfulness of that wicked one who is here only to destroy things that is not his, to slaughter all mankind, and to obliterate the word of God completely from the mind of all soldiers. Therefore Christian soldiers who are dedicated to their superior commander and chief, they must be devoted to the safety and welfare of others, they must continually stand and fight against all of these satanic spirits that is to completely ruin the church of Christ, 2 Tim 2:3-4.

Do you display the characteristic of a Christian? When people are abusing, mistreating and deliberately scandalize your name, do you always modestly behave yourself? Do you always display that submissive spirit of Christ? Do you ever inflict pain on those who injure you? In the mist of it all do your retain your integrity? Do you retaliate, and make the ones repay that you think deserve it? Romans 12:19-21. Friends, by no means take avenge for yourselves, give that over to God, because he said that he will pay back to those who are worthy of it. Do not take the rules into your possession. In its place, nourish your adversary if he is starving, if he is dehydrated give him something to drink, and you will be adding "groups of things on his head." In other words, he will think embarrassed of himself for what he has done to you. Do not allow evil to get the advantage of you, but triumph over evil by you doing them good.

The Bible The Word Of God

The Bible is the World Most Read Book, the World Most Popular Book, the World Most Influential Book, yet it is the World Most Misunderstood Book. The Bible has a total of sixty six (66) books, 39 in the Old Testament, and 27 in the New Testament. Some people say that it was approximately 40 men that wrote the Bible, Heb 1:1.

The Old Testament contains 39 books from Genesis through Malachi.

In the Old Testament, God communicated with the heads of the families through his inspired word which he verbally told the prophets, by which they would transmit verbally and in written letters to the families. The prophets, was men that talked as they were instructed by the heavenly motivation of God, Heb 1:2. The divine inspiration of God did not come into the world by the power of mankind, but mankind got in motion by the Holy Spirit, 2 Peter 1:21. The Old Testament was written so that the people in the New Testament would have a method through the scriptures helping us to learn tolerance to soothe us in times of affliction, distress, and giving us the hope of a better way, Romans 15:4. The Old Testament was our teacher to bring us to Christ the headmaster, educator, guides, and instructor. After Christ came into the world, God moved the Old Testament and the teaching of it out of our way, and gave the world a new promise that is contain in the teaching of the New Testament scriptures, the doctrine of Christ, in which we have the hope of eternal life, Gal 3:24-25. In the Old Testament, God told his people to remove the racket out of their singing, because he did not want to hear the musical sound of their stringed instruments,

Amos 5:23. Furthermore God reprimanded the people for inventing for themselves stringed instruments in the same manner as did David, Amos 6:5.

The New Testament contains 27 books from Matthew through Revelation.

Unlike the Old Testament, The New Testament was paid for with the blood of Jesus Christ, which he gave for the release of all sinners, so that they could be pardon of their sins, Matt 26:28. In the New Testament, God does not talk to the heads of the families through the prophets; rather he talks to us through his son, Jesus Christ, who is the negotiator of a better agreement, and a better guarantee, Heb 8:6. In the New Testament, God gave Christ the authority to transmit his word in any way that was humanly available on the earth, therefore Christ handpicked twelve men that he taught, and instructed in the way of God, they were motivated by the Holy Spirit. Christ gave these men a commandment to go and teach the entire world as it was known unto them verbally, and by writing letters. By these written letters the complete seven continents of the earth, will hear the gospel of Christ. In The New Testament, the Holy Spirit gives Christians the motivation that is beneficial for them to do the good work of God, 2 Tim 3:16-17. In the New Testament, Christians are taught to sing without the use of manmade instruments, they are to sing Holy, and Godly songs to God out of the sincerity of their spirit, Eph 5:19. My Friends, in the New Testament Church, we are to sing and make a wonderful Godly sound unto the Lord. And it is absolutely forbidding for men to use their mouth and create an enjoyable musical sound that the people cannot distantly identify, my brethren this type of singing is a sin in the sight of God. In the church of Christ we are told to sing with the spirit and the understanding, we were not told to sing with mechanical instruments manufactured by men, 1 Cor 14:7-9, 15.

Widows In The Lord's Church

My friends, Widows or women's whose husbands died and they remained unmarried.

My friends, one of the most troubling thing that I have found in the churches of Christ, is the misunderstanding on the subject concerning widows, and widows in deed.

My friends, in the early days of the New Testament, the church was multiplying rapidly and some of the people thought that their widows were being discriminated against during the daily distribution of the food. But the apostles corrected the situation by appointing overseers to be sure that none of the widows would be neglected or overlooked in the daily ministration of the food.

The Bible said, "And in those days, when the number of the disciples was multiplied, there arose a murmuring of the Grecians against the Hebrews, because their widows were neglected in the daily ministration. Then the twelve called the multitude of the disciples unto them, and said, It is not reason that we should leave the word of God, and serve tables. Wherefore, brethren, look ye out among you seven men of honest report, full of the Holy Ghost and wisdom, whom we may appoint over this business" (Acts 6:1-3).

My friends, the Apostles doctrine thoroughly instructed the church concerning the young widows, and it explained in details how to handle this situation.

Paul said, "But the younger widows refuse: for when they have begun to wax wanton against Christ, they will marry" (1 Timothy 5:11).

My friends, Paul explained to Timothy how to take care of the widows who are widows indeed, he gave him step-by-step details on what to look for to make sure that he do it correctly. Paul told Timothy to honor widows that are widows indeed. He told him that if any widows have children or nephews, let them learn first to shew piety at home, and to payback their parents: for that is good and acceptable before God. Paul also told Timothy that a widow indeed, is a widow who is <u>desolate (deserted)</u>, who trusted in God, and continued in appealing to God in prayers night and day. Also Paul told Timothy to make sure that these things are done in order that the widows indeed will be blameless. Furthermore Paul told Timothy to make sure that the widows indeed are at least 60 years old, having been married to only one man. And lastly Paul told Timothy that widows indeed must be will reported of for their good works; if they have brought up children, if they have lodged strangers, if they have washed the saints' feet, if they have relieved the afflicted, if they have diligently followed every good work, after all these principles have been followed by the letter then the congregations who have widows indeed are responsible to take monetary care of those widows. (1 Timothy 5:3-5, 7, 9-10).

My friends, there are congregations of the churches of Christ that are supporting widows financially who are not widows indeed because they has living relatives, congregations are not obligated to assist those widows in any monetary manner, and those congregations that are doing so are in error according to the Scriptures, and the gospel preachers who are allowing that to happen should repent and teach the church the difference between widows and widows indeed, teach them that widows who have living relatives are not widows indeed, teach them that the widow indeed are widows who do not have any living relatives, and do not be ashamed to reiterated to the congregation what Paul said in 1 Timothy chapter 5.

Paul said, "If any man or woman that believeth have widows, let them relieve them, and let not the church be charged; that it may relieve them that are widows indeed" (1 Timothy 5:16).

My friends, there are congregations of the churches of Christ in these days that have hired many false gospel preachers who are nothing but wolves disguised in sheep clothing, who have arranged a bogus plan with their so-called elders and so-called leading brethren, that in case of the local ministers death the congregation would continue to pay the late minister's wife a salary from the church contribution or another plan that they have falsely organized to pay her for the rest of her life.

My friends, those gospel preachers, so-called elders leading brethren's and all who have taken apart in that heinous damnable false doctrine, if they want to be saved must stop following their misguided teaching, which will only lead to condemnation, because their mouths must be stopped.

Paul said, "Whose mouths must be stopped, who subvert whole houses, teaching things which they ought not, for filthy lucre's sake" (Titus 1:11).

My friends, this is a profound example of a family taking care of their widow; there was a man living in a small town with his wife and his two sons. The husband died and his two sons died also and his wife was left a widow, but she had living relatives that live in another town, so she and one of her daughter-in-law went to another town where she has some living relatives, and when they got to the town her relatives to care of them.

The Bible said, "And Naomi had a kinsman of her husband's, a mighty man of wealth, of the family of Elimelech; and his name was Boaz. And Ruth the Moabitess said unto Naomi, Let me now go to the field, and glean ears of corn after him in whose sight I shall find grace. And she said unto her, Go, my daughter" (Ruth 2:1-2).

My friends, the church of Christ is the only church in the world, it holds our salvation, and members of the church should not allow any gospel preacher to jeopardize their souls by allowing them to support widows who are not widows indeed out of the church's money.

Emeritus

My friends, Emeritus is a complimentary title that retired preachers deem excessively important for them to receive a level of respect at which one is regarded by others. It is a man given title that is absolutely against God. Some gospel preachers in the churches of Christ has renounce the fact that wearing titles of man is wrong and yet many gospel preachers are wearing the title Emeritus. These gospel preachers are practicing the very thing they once taught the churches of Christ not to do. All gospel preachers are commanded by God to keep his ordinances as they are written in his word.

Job said, "Let me not, I pray you, accept any man's person, neither let me give flattering titles unto man. For I know not to give flattering titles; in so doing my maker would soon take me away" (Job 32:21-22").

My friends, there is no place in the oracles of God that teach that gospel preachers can retire from preaching, and there is no Scripture in the Bible whatsoever that teach gospel preachers to assumed the title Emeritus. If a gospel preacher has retired from preaching at a particular congregation and is still preaching waiting on a replacement, after the congregation have received another gospel preacher, the retired gospel preacher should at that time stop wearing the title Emeritus.

Peter said, "If any man speak, let him speak as the oracles of God; if any man minister, let him do it as of the ability which God giveth: that God in all things may be glorified through Jesus Christ, to whom be praise and dominion for ever and ever" Amen (1 Peter 4:11).

My friends, the gospel preachers of old, men of renown, obtained the quality of being widely honored by the way they live, and by the way they taught the churches of Christ that the denominational preachers was wrong for wearing title of men, and for being called by God's name "Reverend".

David said, "God sent redemption unto his people: he hath commanded his covenant for ever: holy and reverend is his name" (Psalm 111:9).

My friends, Jesus Christ our master teacher and savior of the world, taught his disciples plainly how not to address the religious Leaders of the churches of Christ nor in the world. Christ particularly told his disciples that all Christians are to be called brothers.

The Bible said, "Don't you be called the chief religious official over all congregations: for one is your highest, Christ Jesus our Lord; and you all are brothers. And do not call any man your spiritual father here on earth: for you have only one spiritual Father, and he is in heaven. And do not be called the highest in rank: for the one who is the highest in rank, and in authority, is Jesus Christ" (Matt 23:8-10).

My friends, there are many gospel preachers nowadays spending so much time trying to make a reputation for themselves, insomuch that they have totally ignored the command of God to preach the word in season and out of season, being patience and kind, because you are trying to build up your brothers that will not listen to the truth of the word, but will go after any strange teaching of men. Furthermore they have forgotten to watch out for the evil things that is out to get them, they also have stopped practicing evangelism, and proving what they say is true. Paul warned the church of Christ at Philippi concerning those who wanted to receive a reputation for themselves.

Paul said, "Let this mind be in you, which was also in Christ Jesus: Who, being in the form of God, thought it not robbery to be equal with God: But made himself of no reputation, and took upon him the form of a servant, and was made in the likeness of men: And being found in fashion as a man, he humbled himself, and became obedient unto death, even the death of the cross" (Philippians 2:5-8).

My friends, all the members of the churches of Christ that live a good Christian life without receiving the glamour, riches, and prosperity that this world have to offer. If they suffer and die for the cause of Jesus Christ and his church that will be good enough to inherit eternal life according to the Scriptures.

John said, "Fear none of those things which thou shalt suffer: behold, the devil shall cast some of you into prison, that ye may be tried; and ye shall have tribulation ten days: be thou faithful unto death, and I will give thee a crown of life" (Revelation 2:10).

My friends, all Christians in the entire world should understand how imperative it is that we live according to the scriptures, so that we will not be tossed and carried about with the false doctrines of men so that when Jesus Christ come we will not be found in error by following the misleading doctrines of men. Furthermore no Christian should by any means be ashamed to be called a Christian. A member of the church of Christ and unquestionably they will not accept or wear any flattering titles of men, not even the title Emeritus. When Jesus Christ was living upon the earth he had a conversation with his disciples concerning the names that the people were calling him, then Peter answered the Lord.

The Bible said, "He saith unto them, But whom say ye that I am? And Simon Peter answered and said, Thou art the Christ, the Son of the living God" (Matthew 16:15-16). Furthermore after Jesus Christ was raised up from the dead he said unto Saul, "I am Jesus of Nazareth". He did not say "I am Emeritus Jesus of Nazareth".

My supplication to all preachers and so-call preachers, males and females, is to renounce all titles of men that you are wearing. Repent and turn to God, because Christ is our example and not man.

Peter said, "For even hereunto were ye called: because Christ also suffered for us, leaving us an example, that ye should follow his steps" (1 Peter 2:21).

Homosexuality Is Absolutely Sinful

Children of God, it is imperative that all bold gospel preachers, and teachers stand firm on the word of God and teach on all of the activities that are going on in the world that is against the word of God which is our religious obligation.

Paul said, "And how I kept back nothing that was profitable unto you, but have shewed you, and have taught you publicly, and from house to house, for I have not shunned to declare unto you all the counsel of God" (Acts 20:20, 27).

All gospel preachers are to prove all things.

Paul said, "Prove all things; hold fast that which is good. Abstain from all appearance of evil" (1 Thess 5:21-22). Therefore it is time to prove that homosexuality is absolutely a sin in the sight of God; it is an ungodly behavior what same sex people do among themselves.

A homosexual person; is a man or woman who is without spiritual morals, who have turned from the natural plan that God put in motion, man with woman, and woman with man. Homosexuals have a lifestyle and social pleasures that only concerns the homosexual group of people. The payments that God have bestowed upon them are multiple types of sexual transmitted viruses and some are fatal.

Homosexuality is absolutely forbidden in the kingdom of God, and should be forbidden in the heart of all mankind.

Paul said, "Rather than to believe what they could recognize was the truth about the word of God; they deliberately made a choice to accept

ROBERT L. PATTERSON

lies. Consequently they offered prayer to the things made by God, but
would not do as they were told by the God who created those things.
Therefore God let them go to do all those immoralities; even their
women twisted themselves against the natural arrangement of God, and
gave themselves to the indulging in homosexuality with one another.
Also the men, in place of having natural sexual intercourse with the
women, they burn up in their twisted minds having sexual desire for
one another, men doing homosexual sins with one another, and for a
reward, and with a penalty they so richly deserved. God will make them
pay by them losing their souls" (Romans 1:25-27).

Homosexual activities reach back as far as the book of Genesis in the Old
Testament. The homosexual behavior at one time was not as openly as it
is today in our society, yet God have never condone this behavior among
mankind, it is immorally wicked, and should forever be incapacitated
forever in the sight of God. Now that people are coming out of the closet,
which is to say coming out of hiding, now publicly man and man or woman
and woman can walk the streets downtown, sit in the parks, hugging and
kissing one another without any form of embarrassment whatsoever.

My friends, homosexuality was an open sin in Sodom, and one day
there came some men to Lot's house, requesting that he would give them
those men that stayed the night with him, that they may do whatsoever
they pleased with them, and Lot pleaded with those men to leave those
men alone and take his daughter's instead but they refused.

The Bible said, "And they called unto Lot, and said unto him, where are
the men which came in to thee this night? bring them out unto us, that
we may know them. And Lot went out at the door unto them, and shut
the door after him, And said, I pray you, brethren, do not so wickedly.
Behold now, I have two daughters which have not known man; let me,
I pray you, bring them out unto you, and do ye to them as is good in
your eyes: only unto these men do nothing; for therefore came they
under the shadow of my roof" (Genesis 19:5-8).

Homosexuality is ridiculously outrageous, it is totally unbelieving that
homosexual women who has been married to a man, and has given

birth to one are more children, has decided that they no longer want to be a wife, nor a mother anymore, so they decided to go through some demonic, damnable transformation, that mentally transformed them from being a woman, and has given them the mental characteristic of a man. What is even more ludicrous, is that even though they make themselves to believe that they have men characteristic, they still have their same woman genitals, the same reproduction mechanism, and their children still called them mother.

The Bible said, "God fashioned man in his structure, in the structure of God fashioned them; man and woman fashioned he them. God hallowed them and God told them to have children, multiply, and fill up the earth and discipline it and he gave him authority over every living thing that move under, over, and upon the earth" (Gen 1:27-28).

Paul warned the church of Christ in Corinth concerning people living immoral lives, he said, "Don't you know that the unrighteous shall not inherit the kingdom of God? Be not deceived: neither fornicators, nor idolaters, nor adulterers, nor effeminate, nor abusers of themselves with mankind, nor thieves, nor covetous, nor drunkards, nor revilers, nor extortioners, shall inherit the kingdom of God. And such were some of you: but ye are washed, but ye are sanctified, but ye are justified in the name of the Lord Jesus, and by the Spirit of our God" (1 Corinthians 6:9-11).

Homosexuality is not a victimless sin in the sight of God. They must turn their life over to God or they will pay the penalty. According to the scriptures, people who live immoral lives will not have any earthly nor heavenly part in the Kingdom of God. My Friends, if you are practicing the role of a homosexual man or woman, then my sincere plead is that you will come out from that life style and turn to God before the end come, so that it will not be said "I never knew you".

The Bible said, "Then said Jesus again unto them, I go my way, and ye shall seek me, and shall die in your sins: whither I go, ye cannot come. I said therefore unto you, that ye shall die in your sins: for if ye believe not that I am he, ye shall die in your sins" (John 8:21-24).

Same Sex Marriage

Marriage is the oldest institution in the world; it was set into motion by the almighty God of heaven. In the beginning God brought a man and a woman together, male and female. God did not bring male and male, or female and female together in marriage for that would have been damnation. God will punish those evil workers of the devil that has given the permission for a man to marry another man, and a woman to marry another woman, for this is another wicked and disgusting thought that man has brought into the world through the lust of the devil.

The Bible said, "And the Lord God caused a deep sleep to fall upon Adam, and he slept: and he took one of his ribs, and closed up the flesh instead thereof; And the rib, which the Lord God had taken from man, made he a woman, and brought her unto the man. And Adam said, This is now bone of my bones, and flesh of my flesh: she shall be called Woman, because she was taken out of Man. Therefore shall a man leave his father and his mother, and shall cleave unto his wife: and they shall be one flesh" (Genesis 2:21-24).

Marriage is a promise that a man and a woman made before God and man that should not be broken, abolished, or put aside by either the husband or the wife without the scriptural authority of Jesus Christ. Married people should honor their marriage and the promises that they made so that their living arrangements will not be dishonored by God.

Paul said, "Know ye not, brethren, (for I speak to them that know the law), how that the law hath dominion over a man as long as he liveth? For the woman which hath an husband is bound by the law to her husband so long as he liveth; but if the husband be dead, she is loosed from the law of her husband. So then if, while her husband liveth, she be married to another man, she shall be called an adulteress: but if her husband be dead, she is free from that law; so that she is no adulteress, though she be married to another man" (Romans 7:1-3).

The Bible said, "They say unto him, Why did Moses then command to give a writing of divorcement, and to put her away? He saith unto them, Moses because of the hardness of your hearts suffered you to put away your wives: but from the beginning it was not so. And I say unto you, Whosoever shall put away his wife, except it be for fornication, and shall marry another, committeth adultery: and whoso marrieth her which is put away doth commit adultery" (Matthew 19:7-9).

Same sex marriage is absolutely sinful, and those that participate in those sinful practices will receive the recompense of their error. Therefore gospel preachers should be given more biblical descriptions on the major role of a husband and a wife, perhaps they should preach more about the first family that God set in place in the Garden of Eden. He also proved to the entire world that in the first family, Adam, He Was the Husband and Father; Eve, She Was the Wife and Mother. Preachers should preach that when two people are having sexual intercourse with each other, it should be done between A Man, (The Husband), And His Wife, (The Woman). Also teach that when Adam and Eve started having children as God commanded them, it was Eve, the wife, the woman that became pregnant and gave birth to their children, and not Adam, the man, the husband, the father.

The Bible said, "And Adam knew Eve his wife; and she conceived, and bare Cain, and said, I have gotten a man from the Lord. And she again bare his brother Abel. And Abel was a keeper of sheep, but Cain was a tiller of the ground" (Genesis 4:1-2).

My friends it is absolutely impossible for two people that have the same type genitals (sexual organs) for either of them to become pregnant, and reproduce, proving that same sex marriage is against the command that God gave to married people when he said to Adam and Eve, "Be fruitful, and multiply, and replenish the earth". Furthermore it is factual that when two men with the same type genitals get involve with having sexual intercourse with each other, one of them have to pretend and act if though his anal canal (his rectum), has been transformed into a woman's vagina, which is morally wrong and disgusting in the sight of God. Also when two women that are married or living together, and is having sexual intercourse with each other is also disgusting, and they all will receive the wrath of God.

The Bible said, "Marriage is honourable in all, and the bed undefiled: but whoremongers and adulterers God will judge" (Hebrews 13:4).

My Friends, I am positively sure that those who are living immoral lives and are having sexual intercourse with a same sex person, is deliberately, and willingly rejecting the word of God, and those unrighteous people will not enter into the kingdom of God, therefore they will have nothing to look forward to after this life is over, but the fiery righteous anger of the almighty God.

The Bible said, "For if we sin wilfully after that we have received the knowledge of the truth, there remaineth no more sacrifice for sins, But a certain fearful looking for of judgment and fiery indignation, which shall devour the adversaries" (Hebrews 10:26-27).

Moses gave Marriage official authority, and our Lord Jesus Christ gave it spiritual, and divine authority, it should be regarded as the Holiest and Happiest relationship among mankind. Marriage should be looked upon as the strength of the church, home, and among our entire civilization. Marriage should be entered into with Godly respect among everyone.

Solomon said, "Whoso fined a wife found a good thing, and obtained favor of the Lord" (Proverbs 18:22).

Making A Request To All Christians Face Book Consumers

My friends, the devil has brought into the world another one of his devilish tricks, that is causing many Christians to become friends with the world through some or all of his electronic website devices that he has developed as a mean to communicate to the entire world. A device that he is using to cause as many Christians that he possibly can to violate the word of God.

John said, "Love not the world, neither the things that are in the world. If any man love the world, the love of the Father is not in him. For all that is in the world, the lust of the flesh, and the lust of the eyes, and the pride of life, is not of the Father, but is of the world. And the world passeth away, and the lust thereof: but he that doeth the will of God abideth for ever" (1 John 2:15-17).

My friends, as a gospel preacher, it is my God given responsibility to warn all Christians that are using Facebook and all other electronic devices, primarily to have casual conversations and sharing their relationship with their worldly friends of the danger they are putting themselves into in the sight of God.

Ezekiel said, "Again, When a righteous man doth turn from his righteousness, and commit iniquity, and I lay a stumblingblock before him, he shall die: because thou hast not given him warning, he shall die in his sin, and his righteousness which he hath done shall not be remembered; but his blood will I require at thine hand. Nevertheless if thou warn the righteous man, that the righteous sin not, and he doth not sin, he shall surely live, because he is warned; also thou hast delivered thy soul" (Ezek 3:20-21).

My friends, my question is to all Christians that are using Facebook and other electronic devices, are all of your friend's members of the church of Christ? Are they faithful in the church? Are they proving what the will of the Lord is? And do all of your friends love and obey the Lord?

James said, "Ye adulterers and adulteresses, know ye not that the friendship of the world is enmity with God? whosoever therefore will be a friend of the world is the enemy of God. Do ye think that the scripture saith in vain, The spirit that dwelleth in us lusteth to envy"? (James 4:4-5).

My friends, I truly hope that as Christians you have enough remembrance of God's word in you to know that, when Christians are fellowshipping with none Christians by any means they are not doing the will of God, therefore they are in sin. If you have friends in the world that do not believe in the church of Christ, then they are in darkness, and your responsibility to those unbelievers is to teach them out of darkness.

Paul said, "And have no fellowship with the unfruitful works of darkness, but rather reprove them. For it is a shame even to speak of those things which are done of them in secret" (Eph 5:11-12).

My friends, when Christians are in the comfort of their own home and are communicating verbally, or by way of the web-site with their friends, who are not Christians, members of the churches of Christ and they should know the consequences of going against what the Bible teach concerning having friendship with the world?

The Bible said, "For if we go on sinning deliberately after receiving the knowledge of the truth, there no longer remains a sacrifice for sins, but a fearful expectation of judgment, and a fury of fire that will consume the adversaries" (Hebrews 10:26-27).

My Friends, one of the most crippling things to the world and to the churches of Christ concerning these "web-site" consumers, is that there are so many gospel preachers using it, and instead of teaching the gospel of Christ to those that they are communicating with, they have involved themselves and are participating in the same sinful activities that the world and some of the unfaithful Christians are doing.

Peter said, "For if after they have escaped the pollutions of the world through the knowledge of the Lord and Saviour Jesus Christ, they are again entangled therein, and overcome, the latter end is worse with them than the beginning. For it had been better for them not to have known the way of righteousness, than, after they have known it, to turn from the holy commandment delivered unto them. But it is happened unto them according to the true proverb, The dog is turned to his own vomit again; and the sow that was washed to her wallowing in the mire" (2 Peter 2:20-22).

My friends, this request is to help Christians, and all mankind all over the world to realize that it is high time for all to turn from those sinful pleasures that the devil have given for the world to enjoy in this present world of darkness before God give all of the sinful workers of pleasure up to a worthless mind, and allow them to think continually of new ways of sinning, and then condemn them for doing so. I sincerely hope that you will put your faith and your face in the book of the Lord so that you may save yourselves from dying in your sins. Please take heed all of you "web-site" consumers, get your lives in order before you die, because the Lord will come without warning. Paul made a heartfelt plead to the Christians in the church of Christ in Corinth.

Paul said, "Don't join with none Christians: for what friendship does the righteous have with none righteous? And what spiritual union does the people of light have with the people of darkness? Therefore come out and separate yourself from them, the Lord said, and do not become a part of these contaminated thing and I will delivery you, And I will be a God to you, and you shall be my children, said the Almighty God" (2 Cor 6:14, 17-18).

My friends, my prayerful plead to the God of heaven is that all Christians "web-site" consumers, would reevaluate their spiritual responsibility to

God, and to the world. I am also pleading to all gospel preachers who are "web-site" consumers to repent and ask God to forgive them, and to open their understanding so that they may understand the statement that Jesus made so vividly clear to them in John chapter 8.

John said, "Then said Jesus again unto them, I go my way, and ye shall seek me, and shall die in your sins: whither I go, ye cannot come" (John 8:21).

The Churches Of Christ Needs Faithful Spiritual Minded Gospel Preachers

My friends, the churches of Christ needs faithful Spiritual minded gospel preachers who can teach and train new Christian men as soon as they are baptized how to be Christians soldiers. These men must be train similar to an athlete, because for an athlete to win a gold medal, they must start at a very young age, they must train hard and long. Athletes are trained to win championships. Teach them that they can reach the highest level of accomplishment and that they will triumphant in the Lord Jesus Christ.

My friends, Jethro, Moses father-in-law, instructed him to find able or capable men that was able to learn, teach the ordinance of God, and men that love the righteousness of God. Jethro told Moses that when he had finished training those men to put them over different size groups that they may teach them, Exodus 18:19-24. Paul gave Timothy and Titus the same type of responsibilities that Jethro gave Moses in the wilderness.

Paul said to Timothy, "Thou therefore, my son, be strong in the grace that is in Christ Jesus. And the things that thou hast heard of me among many witnesses, the same commit thou to faithful men, who shall be able to teach others also. Thou therefore endure hardness, as a good soldier of Jesus Christ" (2 Tim 2:1-3).

Also Paul said to Titus, "For this cause left I thee in Crete, that thou shouldest set in order the things that are wanting, and ordain elders in every city, as I had appointed thee" (Titus 1:5).

My friends, the churches of Christ needs faithful Spiritual minded gospel preachers who will teach men to keep the ordinances of God just as Jethro told Moses in the wilderness and as Paul told Timothy and Titus in the church, and neither of those men was told to allow women to teach over or within any group of the people of God in the wilderness, neither in any congregation of the churches of Christ.

Paul said, "Be ye followers of me, even as I also am of Christ. Now I praise you, brethren, that ye remember me in all things, and keep the ordinances, as I delivered them to you. But I would have you know, that the head of every man is Christ; and the head of the woman is the man; and the head of Christ is God" (1 Corinthians 11:1-3).

Furthermore Paul said, "But I suffer not a woman to teach, nor to usurp authority over the man, but to be in silence" (1 Timothy 2:12).

My friends, the churches of Christ needs faithful Spiritual minded gospel preachers who are dedicated and working themselves, and teaching the men to study the word of God so they will grow and become physically, mentally, and spiritually able to perform the task that the Lord has instructed the church to do. Teach them not to allow anything that the devil can do to hinder or cause them to stop working for the Lord, regardless of the suffering, the anguish, the harassment, or threats that he may put in their way. Let those men know that the task that is set before them is tedious, and the enemy is strong, but if they will stand still, and fight together they will receive the victory.

Solomon said, "Two are better than one; because they have a good reward for their labour. For if they fall, the one will lift up his fellow: but woe to him that is alone when he falleth; for he hath not another to help him up. And if one prevail against him, two shall withstand him; and a threefold cord is not quickly broken" (Ecclesiastes 4:9-10, 12).

My friends, the churches of Christ needs faithful Spiritual minded gospel preachers who will take the leadership position that the Holy Ghost appointed them, and will keep the board of trustees and other so-called church leaders that the congregation has appointed in their place according to the scriptures.

Paul said, "Yea, ye yourselves know, that these hands have ministered unto my necessities, and to them that were with me. I have shewed you all things, how that so labouring ye ought to support the weak, and to remember the words of the Lord Jesus, how he said, It is more blessed to give than to receive" (Acts 20:34-35).

My friends, the churches of Christ needs Spiritual minded gospel preachers who will train men to carry out the word of God in the churches of Christ as Moses did in the wilderness and as Paul told Timothy to do.

Paul said, "I press toward the mark for the prize of the high calling of God in Christ Jesus. Let us therefore, as many as be perfect, be thus minded: and if in any thing ye be otherwise minded, God shall reveal even this unto you. Nevertheless, whereto we have already attained, let us walk by the same rule, let us mind the same thing" (Philippians 3:14-16).

My friends, the churches of Christ needs Spiritual minded gospel preachers who will teach men not become weary or disgusted in their mind.

Paul said, "And let us not be weary in well doing: for in due season we shall reap, if we faint not" (Galatians 6:9).

Also Paul said, "I have gain the power over the adversary, I have completed the program, I have maintained the confidence: From this time forth there is a crown of righteousness waiting for me, that the Lord, the righteous mediator, will give me at the last day: and not only to me, for also he will give it to all them who are looking for him at the finish line, when this life is over" (2 Tim 4:7-8).

Church Autonomy

My friends, Autonomy mean independent, self-governing, and supreme; and to better understand the individuality of the churches of Christ, we must understand that each congregation of the churches of Christ is autonomous, and independent of itself, it is absolutely not governed by a group of church ministers and brethren. Therefore since each congregation of the churches of Christ is autonomous, they should carry out the work that God have put in their trust without the collaboration the leaders of other congregations.

Jesus said, "If ye love me, keep my commandments. Jesus answered and said unto him, If a man love me, he will keep my words: and my Father will love him, and we will come unto him, and make our abode with him" (John 14:15, 23).

My friends, the Lord promised to build only one church, his church the church of Christ.

Christ said, "Upon this bedrock truth I will construct my church" (Matt 16:18).

My friends, the word my church signified that it belongs to Christ and the church of Christ is the only thing of its kind that cannot be duplicated, and it is autonomous, the scripture teaches that when the end come Christ will transport the kingdom up to God.

Paul said, "Then cometh the end, when he shall have delivered up the kingdom to God, even the Father; when he shall have put down all rule and all authority and power" (1 Corinthians 15:24).

My friends, church autonomy does not mean that church members are not to fellowship with one another, on the contrary Christians should fellowship with one another. The fact of the matter is that each congregation of the churches of Christ should be operating within their own means, without receiving regular monetary assistant from other congregations. Furthermore Preachers who have the ability start a congregation must know that the congregation the adequate income to sustain that work,

Luke said, "For which of you, intending to build a tower, sitteth not down first, and counteth the cost, whether he have sufficient to finish it"? (Luke 14:28)

My friends, to help us to further understand the autonomy of the churches of Christ, we need to understand what John told the "seven congregations that was in the region of Asia" (Rev 1:4).

My friends, when the New Testament was written, and as the gospel was being preached many different people was becoming Disciples of Christ. There was many people being baptized, some of them was unlearned and ignorant men that did not have any previous knowledge of God. Therefore they started indulging in many sinful pleasures, some of the congregations were allowing people to perform sexual act openly without being reprimanded, and some were even worshipping Satan.

The Bible said, "Notwithstanding I have a few things against thee, because thou sufferest that woman Jezebel, which calleth herself a prophetess, to teach and to seduce my servants to commit fornication, and to eat things sacrificed unto idols" (Revelation 2:20).

My friends, in the book of Revelation we find in the doctrine of John, that there were seven congregation, and seven angels, and no place in the doctrine of John did tell any of those seven angels to come together and discuss how they were to handle their individual responsibility, John told each congregation what they must do to resolve their own problems among themselves.

The Bible said, "Remember therefore from whence thou art fallen, and repent, and do the first works; or else I will come unto thee quickly, and will remove thy candlestick out of his place, except thou repent" (Revelation 2:5). Even though those seven churches of Christ in Asia was autonomous and had a different set of problems their individual responsibility was to correct them and to repent.

Paul said, "For whatsoever things were written aforetime were written for our learning, that we through patience and comfort of the scriptures might have hope" (Romans 15:4).

Furthermore Paul said, "Now I beseech you, brethren, by the name of our Lord Jesus Christ, that ye all speak the same thing, and that there be no divisions among you; but that ye be perfectly joined together in the same mind and in the same judgment" (1 Corinthians 1:10).

Still Paul said, "All scripture is given by inspiration of God, and is profitable for doctrine, for reproof, for correction, for instruction in righteousness: That the man of God may be perfect, thoroughly furnished unto all good works" (2 Timothy 3:16-17).

My friends, I cannot understand why some gospel preachers would allow other gospel preachers to persuade them to go against the doctrine of Christ and formulate a monthly meeting structured to discuss the business and problems of other congregations, after knowing what Paul taught the church at Rome, the church at Corinth, and what he taught Timothy.

My friends, in the churches of Christ in Asia each congregation had only one guardian angel over it to oversee the things that was happening in it.

My friends, my prayers to God is that after you have read this epistle, that you will honestly examine yourself and see if you are in violation of the doctrine of Christ, and if so I pray that you will repent, and that you will always remember what Peter said in 1 peter 4.

Peter said, "If any man speak, let him speak as the oracles of God; if any man minister, let him do it as of the ability which God giveth: that God in all things may be glorified through Jesus Christ, to whom be praise and dominion for ever and ever" Amen (1 Peter 4:11).

The Misunderstanding Of Elders In The Churches Of Christ

My friends, the misunderstanding on the subject of elders in the churches of Christ in the last days is because many gospel preachers will not explain to the churches of Christ that after the apostles died, some previous things in the church was going to cease, or vanish away, such as the miracles of laying on of hands and imparting spiritual gifts to others, and the ordaining of elders in the church, because there is no one on earth with the authoritative power of the Holy Ghost who can lay hands on someone and impart spiritual gifts unto them. Paul said, "Charity never faileth: but whether there be prophecies, they shall fail; whether there be tongues, they shall cease; whether there be knowledge, it shall vanish away" (1 Corinthians 13:8).

My friends, during the days when the apostles lived upon the earth, the Hebrews writer wrote to the Hebrews telling them about their comrades, the apostles, prophets, gospel preachers, bishops, and elders; those men who was presently preaching to them the word of God, he told them to surrender themselves to those men because they was watching for their souls. The Bible said, "Remember them which have the rule over you, who have spoken unto you the word of God: whose faith follow, considering the end of their conversation. Obey them that have the rule over you, and submit yourselves: for they watch for your souls, as they that must give account, that they may do it with joy, and not with grief: for that is unprofitable for you. Know you that our brother Timothy is set at liberty; with whom, if he comes shortly, I will see you. Salute all them that have the rule over you, and all the saints. They of Italy salute you" (Hebrews 13:7, 17, 23-24).

My Friends, please listen to me with an open mind, because before there was a church of Christ in the world, there were elders who was the overseers of their flocks. Paul was in a town called Miletus, he "sent for the elders of the church in Ephesus" (Acts 20:17). Those elders that Paul summoned to meet him in Miletus were elders of the church overseers of their flocks before they came to meet Paul in Miletus. In Miletus, Paul ordained those elders through the power of the Holy Ghost to be the spiritual overseers of their flocks and with the ability to teach the word of God. Paul said the those elders, "Take heed therefore unto yourselves, and to all the flock, over the which the Holy Ghost hath made you overseers, to feed the church of God, which he hath purchased with his own blood" (Acts 20:28).

My Friends, Paul gave Timothy a different responsibility than he gave the elders from Ephesus, he did not ordain Timothy to be an elder over a flock. Paul said to Timothy, "I charge thee therefore before God, and the Lord Jesus Christ, who shall judge the quick and the dead at his appearing and his kingdom; Preach the word; be instant in season, out of season; reprove, rebuke, exhort with all long suffering and doctrine" (2 Timothy 4:1-2).

My friends, Paul gave Titus the responsibility to arrange everything that will not stand up to standards, and to ordain elders in every city, but Paul did not ordain Titus to be an elder over a flock. Paul said to Titus, "For this cause left I thee in Crete, that thou shouldest set in order the things that are wanting, and ordain elders in every city, as I had appointed thee" (Titus 1:5).

My friends, it is totally ludicrous for gospel preachers to believe that they can be gospel preachers of the churches of Christ who have been sent by God to set things in order, and at the same time be ordained by the power of the Holy Spirit to be an elder to oversee the church, that is absolutely misleading, those gospel preachers only want to act if though they are the Generals over the inheritance of God. John said, "I wrote unto the church: but Diotrephes, who loveth to have the preeminence among them, receiveth us not. Wherefore, if I come, I will remember his deeds which he doeth, prating against us with malicious words: and not content therewith, neither doth he himself receive the brethren, and forbiddeth them that would, and casteth them out of the church" (3 John 9-10).

My friends, there are some gospel preachers who have made for themselves dual roles in some of the congregations of the church, one as a gospel preacher, and one as an ordained elder, that is totally misleading, simply because of their misunderstanding of the greeting that Peter made when he met with those elders of the church, whom he ordained by the power of the Holy Ghost and made them to be the spiritual overseers of their flocks, and with the ability to teach the word of God. Peter said, "The elders which are among you I exhort, who am also an elder, and a witness of the sufferings of Christ, and also a partaker of the glory that shall be revealed: Feed the flock of God which is among you, taking the oversight thereof, not by constraint, but willingly; not for filthy lucre, but of a ready mind; Neither as being lords over God's heritage, but being examples to the flock" (1 Peter 5:1-3).

My friends, Paul taught Timothy in his doctrine to be examples of those that believe, and he never told Timothy that he could retire from preaching the word of God. Paul said, "Let no man despise thy youth; but be thou an example of the believers, in word, in conversation, in charity, in spirit, in faith, in purity. Till I come, give attendance to reading, to exhortation, to doctrine" (1Tim 4:12-13).

My friends, Paul told the church of Christ in Thessalonica that they must prove all things when it comes to God's word, and he warned them to stay away from the things that can develop into sin, and yet Paul never told them that the preachers can retire from preaching the gospel of Christ. Paul said, "Prove all things; hold fast that which is good. Abstain from all appearance of evil" (1 Thess 5:21-22).

My friends, the prophet Jeremiah had become so disgusted with the people of God until he decided to stop preaching on his own will, but God caused something to happen in his soul that caused him to realize the danger that he had put himself in for having the notion to stop preaching the word of God. Perhaps if all gospel preachers who have retired from preaching the gospel of Christ, and those who are planning on retiring from preaching the gospel of Christ, would consider that they are in a position that God put them in, and that he is the only one that should be able to stop them from doing what he has called them to do, then maybe they will move the thought of retiring from their minds, and will remember and follow the concept of Jeremiah when he wanted to stop preaching the word of God. Jeremiah said, "For since I spake, I cried out, I cried violence and spoil; because the word of the LORD was made a reproach unto me, and a derision, daily. Then I said, I will not make mention of him, nor speak any more in his name. But his word was in mine heart as a burning fire shut up in my bones, and I was weary with forbearing, and I could not stay" (Jer 20:8-9).

My friends, at the age of 12 years old Jesus told his parents that he must be about his father's business. Jesus said, "And he said unto them, How is it that ye sought me? wist ye not that I must be about my Father's business"? (Luke 2:49). And for the next 18 to 24 years Jesus worked for God. Jesus was approximately 32 to 36 years old when he died.

My friends, Jesus explained to his disciples that he had to work while he was alive, because after death he can no longer work for God on the earth. Jesus said, "I must work the works of him that sent me, while it is day: the night cometh, when no man can work" (John 9:4).

My friends, Solomon gave an analogy to the people of God in the Old Testament which is for our learning, he explained to the people that when they start working for God they must do it with all their strength, he also told them that they must do it until they die. The Bible said, "Whatsoever thy hand findeth to do, do it with thy might; for there is no work, nor device, nor knowledge, nor wisdom, in the grave, whither thou goest" (Ecclesiastes 9:10).

My friends, the prophets that God called to preach for him, preached for him until death, Jesus Christ was sent by God to work for him, and he worked for God until death; the apostles of Christ was sent by Christ to preach the gospel of Christ until death.

My friends, many gospel preachers who have been called and sent by God to preach the gospel of Christ until death, have no doubt allowed their father the devil to stop them from preaching the gospel of Christ before they die, and caused them to believe that they can retire from preaching the gospel of Christ, and to eat, drink, and be happy for the rest of their lives? Luke said, "And Jesus said unto him, No man, having put his hand to the plough, and looking back, is fit for the kingdom of God" (Luke 9:62).

My friends, I went to work on the railroad there was a ratio that the workers had to meet before they were eligible for retirement, the ratio was that the employee had to work for the company

30 years, and they had to be 60 years old to qualify for retirement.

My friends, there is only one ratio that the Bible have in place for gospel preachers, that is death, Paul explained to Timothy the seriousness, and the reality of being a faithful gospel preacher until death. Paul said, "I have fought a good fight, I have finished my course, I have kept the faith: Henceforth there is laid up for me a crown of righteousness, which the Lord, the righteous judge, shall give me at that day: and not to me only, but unto all them also that love his appearing" (2 Timothy 4:7-8).

My friends, all gospel preachers who are ordaining men in their congregations and calling them elders are doing so contrary to sound doctrine and without the authoritative power of the Holy Ghost, and if these gospel preachers do not stop this senseless misunderstanding of the word elders, they will receive to themselves the recompense of their error if they do not repent.

My friends, Paul said in Galatians 4:16 "Am I therefore become your enemy, because I tell you the truth?" I also want to say as the apostle Paul said, "Am I therefore become your enemy, because I tell you the truth"?

Little Children

My friends, in the beginning, the God of heaven created man and woman, he brought them together as husband and wife, the first family on the earth. He gave them a commandment to have children and to fill the whole earth. All families should be governed by the word of God and all children are to be born in a home with a father and mother that is married to each other, which is God's will.

The Bible said, "So God created man in his own image, in the image of God created he him; male and female created he them. And God blessed them, and God said unto them, Be fruitful, and multiply, and replenish the earth, and subdue it: and have dominion over the fish of the sea, and over the fowl of the air, and over every living thing that moveth upon the earth" (Genesis 1:27-28).

My friends, a young married man is happy when he have children born to him by his wife, it's like a hunter with his bag full of sharply pointed arrows to protect himself, and because he will have someone to help him if trouble should come.

The Bible said, "As arrows are in the hand of a mighty man; so are children of the youth. Happy is the man that hath his quiver full of them: they shall not be ashamed, but they shall speak with the enemies in the gate" (Psalm 127:4-5).

My friends, God gave the responsibility to parents to teach their children about him and his son Jesus Christ, so they will grow up in the knowledge of him. Moses told Israel they should love the LORD their God with their complete mind, with their complete spirit, and do it with all of their strength.

The Bible said, "These are the words that Moses gave them, he also gave them a command to do it immediately, they shall remain in their heart, he told them to teach these commands thoroughly to their children, you must talk about them when you in sitting down at home, when you are waking along the way, when you go to bed at night, and when you get up in the morning" (Deut 6:5-7).

My friends, there should not be any doubt in our minds that God want all the children of the world to know him. Parents are the mediators between their children and God, until the children come into the age of accountability which varies from child to child. Therefore all parents should raise their children in the manner that God required, so that when they do reach the age of accountability they will be knowledgeable enough to follow the word of God for the remaining of their lives.

Salomon said, "Train up a child in the way he should go: and when he is old, he will not depart from it" (Proverbs 22:6).

My friends, all children should be born in a spiritual family, they should be sheltered, secured, and protected from all types of dangers and abuses that so often shatters and destroys their little weak minds. Parents that are living with an abusive person should remove themselves and their children out of harm's way, and immediately report that abusive person to the law officers, because children have social and civil rights, and should be given the privilege to grow up in a care free environment. Children should be able to attend school without fear of being abducted by anyone. If a known pedophile is living in or near your community, it is your responsibility to report this person to the authority as soon as possible.

My friends, children are born in a state of innocence, and it is imperative that all parents support them as they grow into adulthood. Teach them how to love their mother, father, and their entire family. Parents should never leave their children alone allowing them to grow up on their own, because children cannot properly teach and raise themselves. Again it is a God given responsibility to married males and females, husbands and wives, and fathers we have a grave accountability, because we are to bring up our children in the protection of the Lord.

Paul said, "Bring up our children helping them to grow and to develop into the kind, and earnest reproof of the Lord" (Eph 6:4).

My friends, fathers are to teach their children to listen to their teaching, and to never abandon the principle of their mother.

Salomon said, "My son, hear the instruction of thy father, and forsake not the law of thy mother" (Prov 1:8).

My friends, parents, teach your children that if the street group come after them to become a part of their group, teach them that if this should happen to them to turn from them.

Salomon said, "My son, if sinners entice thee, consent thou not" (Prov 1:10).

My friends, parents, teach your children that there will come a time when they must separate from childhood and become adults. When this transformation take place, the children that have grown up with the proper teaching and training from their parents, and with the help of God will make this transition successfully. Teach them to always remember that they can live a long good life upon the earth.

Paul said, "When I was a child, I spake as a child, I understood as a child, I thought as a child: but when I became a man, I put away childish things" (1 Cor 13:11).

My friends, my prayers to God is that after you have read this epistle, you will honestly examine yourself and see if you are the parents, or parent that God require you to be, and if not please make the necessary corrections before it is too late.

Paul said, "Be ye followers of me, even as I also am of Christ. Now I praise you, brethren, that ye remember me in all things, and keep the ordinances, as I delivered them to you. But I would have you know, that the head of every man is Christ; and the head of the woman is the man; and the head of Christ is God" (1 Corinthians 11:1-3).

Some Things Women Can Do
In The Church

My friends, the apostles in the New Testament did not give a description on the responsibility of women and worship in the churches of Christ. Many Christians misunderstand the word church to mean the church building, many misunderstand church business meetings versus church worship. Paul told Timothy that the women are to be quiet in the church business, for women was never allowed to speak over the men.

Paul said, "But I suffer not a woman to teach, nor to usurp authority over the man, but to be in silence" (1 Timothy 2:12).

My friends, in worship services women can sing, but there are men leading the song services, when men stand and say to the congregation, let us pray, don't that include women also? Yet men are leading the prayers, women can say amen in worship services, in Ephesians 5, Paul did not tell the women in the church at Ephesus not to sing in worship services.

Paul said, "Speaking to yourselves in psalms and hymns and spiritual songs, singing and making melody in your heart to the Lord" (Ephesians 5:19).

My friends, all the things that the church do in business meetings, and in worship services must be done decently and in the order that is described by the Bible.

Paul said, "Let all things be done decently and in order" (1 Corinthians 14:40).

Furthermore Paul said, "For Adam was first formed, then Eve. And Adam was not deceived, but the woman being deceived was in the transgression" (1 Timothy 2:13-14).

My friends, women was cursed by God to be under obedience to the husbands, and they would have pain in childbearing, all because of her disobedient to her husband.

The Bible said, "Unto the woman he said, I will greatly multiply thy sorrow and thy conception; in sorrow thou shalt bring forth children; and thy desire shall be to thy husband, and he shall rule over thee. And unto Adam he said, Because thou hast hearkened unto the voice of thy wife, and hast eaten of the tree, of which I commanded thee, saying, Thou shalt not eat of it: cursed is the ground for thy sake; in sorrow shalt thou eat of it all the days of thy life" (Genesis 3:16-17).

My friends, since the days of Adam and Eve women have become what they call liberated, which mean that they can do things by their own way of thinking, and through the women liberation movement they took on the same responsibility as men, which even in these days is contrary to the law of God. Paul explained this in details to the church of Christ in Corinth.

Paul said, "Now I praise you, brethren, that ye remember me in all things, and keep the ordinances, as I delivered them to you. But I would have you know, that the head of every man is Christ; and the head of the woman is the man; and the head of Christ is God" (1 Corinthians 11:2-3).

My friends, when the word church is used it does not only mean congregation, women in the church can teach young wives how to love and follow their husbands, they have the responsibility to teach the young married women their role in the home, and how to carry themselves, they must also teach the young married women to devote their time concentrating on the things they can do to please the Lord without distraction.

Paul said, "That they may teach the young women to be sober, to love their husbands, to love their children, To be discreet, chaste, keepers at home, good, obedient to their own husbands, that the word of God be not blasphemed" (Titus 2:4-5).

Also Paul said, "There is difference also between a wife and a virgin. The unmarried woman careth for the things of the Lord, that she may be holy both in body and in spirit: but she that is married careth for the things of the world, how she may please her husband" (1 Corinthians 7:34-35).

My friends, the apostle Paul gave a great amount of gratitude to the women of the churches of Christ, he call many of them by name, women who have work hard in the church, helping others, and one women he made special attention to, who had performed many services for Paul and others, yet there is no recording whatsoever of any of these women working within any of the congregations of the churches of Christ that Paul attended.

Paul said, "I commend unto you Phebe our sister, which is a servant of the church which is at Cenchrea: That ye receive her in the Lord, as becometh saints, and that ye assist her in whatsoever business she hath need of you: for she hath been a succourer of many, and of myself also" (Romans 16:1-2).

My friends, some gospel preachers are allowing women from their congregations to speak at other congregations on what they call ladies day lectureship, and still tell these same women to keep silent in the church.

There is no place in the Scriptures that God, Jesus Christ, or any of his apostles ever gave gospel preachers the authority to allow women to teach or preach in any congregation of the churches of Christ.

My friends, it is time for all gospel preachers to stop living in the Neanderthal or primitive age, and start teaching the truth concerning the role of women in the churches of Christ.

My friends, all Christians have been instructed to read and learn the Holy Scriptures for themselves, so that they will be accepted before God.

Paul said, "Study to shew thyself approved unto God, a workman that needeth not to be ashamed, rightly dividing the word of truth" (2 Tim 2:15).

Contrary Christians

My friends, children are born without their own individual set of values, therefore as children grow they develop their own values, and when they start working trying to achieve their goals in life, suddenly without warning from out of the blue everything appears to have turned upside down complete opposite of what they suspected; normally children values are brought on by their parents.

Paul said, "When I call to remembrance the unfeigned faith that is in thee, which dwelt first in thy grandmother Lois, and thy mother Eunice; and I am persuaded that in thee also" (2 Timothy 1:5).

My friends, life does not have a book of rules, or a set of standards written to teach us how to expect the unexpected brought on by an act of nature. Therefore we give thanks to the God of heaven for giving the church and the world a book of rules, and standards that will lead us safely through the expected and unexpected things that we must go through in this life.

The Bible said, "Seek ye out of the book of the Lord, and read: no one of these shall fail, none shall want her mate: for my mouth it hath commanded, and his spirit it hath gathered them" (Isaiah 34:16).

My friends, all Christians must realize and be prepared for there are many different problems that are going to come our way; nevertheless we must never allow the works of the devil to cause us to go contrary to the word of God. The devil is a deceiver, and he uses his lustful worldly desires by persuading Christians to abandon their first love.

John said, "Nevertheless I have somewhat against thee, because thou hast left thy first love" (Revelation 2:4).

My friends, there are some gospel preachers in the church of Christ who love to work for God, but when the devil come in causing problems among the members, instead of the preacher and members working together to resolve the problems, some preachers will allowed the devil to cause them to go contrary to the Holy Spirit and cause some of their members to abandon their congregations, John the Revelator gave some warnings to Christians.

Paul said, "For I know this, that after my departing shall grievous wolves enter in among you, not sparing the flock" (Acts 20:29).

My friends, most God fearing parents do their best to raise and guide their children in the best Godly surroundings as humanly possible for the sake of their children; they will always stand guard against the evil workers of darkness that is always trying to win them over, good parents will not leave because of hard times, instead they will stand and defend their children and positively will never leave them out in the world allowing the devil to come and destroy their souls.

John said, "Do not be frightened by what you are going to experience in your life, because of the devil, fore he will cause many people to lose their souls. Christians will be mistreated for a short period of time. Continue to be devoted even if it mean that you must give up your life, for if you do you will gain an everlasting life" (Rev 2:10).

My friends, some parents do their very best to save their children from harm, and as heart breaking as it is many of our young Christians have totally abandoned the church and have gone contrary to Christ and his church. Some of the young Christians have started living in all kind of rebellion and immoral behaviors, some of our young men and women are experiencing homosexual pleasure with other men and women, some young men are living with women in a premarital arrangement, and giving birth to illegitimate babies as if they were legally married.

Paul said, "Now concerning the things whereof ye wrote unto me: It is good for a man not to touch a woman. Nevertheless, to avoid fornication, let every man have his own wife, and let every woman have her own husband" (1 Corinthians 7:1-2).

My friends, many parents treat and respect the awful sinful living arrangements that their children are living with their unlawful companions, giving young men and women more ground to freely explore the highest level of their sinful imagination, believing that they have a blessing from their parents, saying that it is all right to live in this type of a predicament, totally leaving these young people up to believing that they can live a carefree life free from any type of spiritual guidance from the word of God without any repercussion from the Lord whatsoever.

Isaiah said, "The wicked should leave behind their wrong way of living, and their way of thinking, and return unto the Lord, for God will have mercy upon all them that will repent, and turn to him from all their wrong doing" (Isaiah 55:7).

Alcoholic Drinking

My friends, when Jesus was living in the world, he proved himself to be the son of God by many infallible proofs, his first proof was when he turned water into wine, the wine that Jesus made was fresh crushed grape juice not old fermented wine that would cause people to get drunk unless they drink it excessively.

John said, "And he saith unto them, Draw out now, and bear unto the governor of the feast. And they bare it. When the ruler of the feast had tasted the water that was made wine, and knew not whence it was: (but the servants which drew the water knew;) the governor of the feast called the bridegroom" (John 2:8-9).

My friends, it is imperative that all people of the world learn that God have always commanded his spiritual leaders to teach his people the dissimilarity concerning what is spiritual and what is not spiritual. And by all means drinking fermented drinks is not a Spiritual thing in the sight of God.

The Bible said, "And they shall teach my people the difference between the holy and profane, and cause them to discern between the unclean and the clean, (Ezekiel 44:23).

My friends, God told Moses that the people of Israel was acting like those people that lived in the towns of "Sodom and Gomorrah", who did some very bad acidic things that would kill people, those people would get drunk and rape males and females alike, they would drink so much wine and fermented drinks until they would pass out, and sometime when they awoke the next day they would not even realize what they had done the night before, this fact is proven with Lot and his two daughters.

The Bible said, "And they made their father drink wine that night: and the firstborn went in, and lay with her father; and he perceived not when she lay down, nor when she arose. And they made their father drink wine that night also: and the younger arose, and lay with him; and he perceived not when she lay down, nor when she arose. Thus were both the daughters of Lot with child by their father" (Genesis 19:32-36).

My friends, fermented drinking can give people a false conception of their environment, which have caused many people to lose their friends, love ones, and their families. Have you ever stopped and wondered why is it that so often in a fatal automobile accident that involves a drunk driver the drunk driver is the one who walks away? Drinking fermented drinks have fooled people into thinking they can drink alcoholic drinks and still perform rationally. My friends believe me, that is never the case, because the people that drink fermented drinks are often frustrated, because strong drink can overpower people and send them into an explosive rage that make them act totally out of character.

Solomon said, "Wine is a mocker, strong drink is raging: and whosoever is deceived thereby is not wise" (Proverbs 20:1).

John the Revelator, revealed the divine word of God to his people, these same people criticize him saying that he had a demonic spirit, and he was exile to an island the people called Patmos.

The Bible said, "For John came neither eating nor drinking, and they say, He hath a devil" (Matt 11:18).

My friends, the same people that criticized John, criticized Jesus saying that he was an "excessive over eater and a public drunk" and they crucified him on a cross.

The Bible said, "The Son of man came eating and drinking, and they say, Behold a man gluttonous, and a winebibber, a friend of publicans and sinners. But wisdom is justified of her children. Then began he to upbraid the cities wherein most of his mighty works were done, because they repented not" (Matt 11:19-20).

My friends, there are people that you tell the truth, and you will have to receive repercussion from those same people. After looking closely at the way the people treated the apostle John, and Jesus Christ the savior of the world, that really helped me to better understand what Paul meant when he penned these words, "have I made myself your adversary, by me telling nothing but truth to you all"? (Gal 4:16).

My friends, drinking fermented drinks can cause a great deal of risk to a pregnant woman unborn child, it can cause damage to the unborn child, also it can cause the child to have a physical and psychological imbalance after it is born. Drinking fermented drinks is detrimental to our family and friends, drinking fermented drinks has caused many life changing problems, it has destroyed many homes, it has caused the loss of many innocent people lives, it has caused many so-called Christians to think that it is all right to drink sociably in the privacy of their homes, and this list goes on and on with no end in sight. Therefore, the only way to destroy these heinous demonic behaviors of the devil is to listen to what the word of God say concerning drinking fermented drinks.

My Friends, drinking fermented drinks is not a righteous or a wise thing to do according to the scriptures. Solomon said, "Fermented drinking is not for kings, O Lemuel, for it is not for kings to drink fermented wine, and it is not for a member of a royal family to drink intoxicating drinks, unless they drink, and cannot remember the commandments of the Lord, and be impaired in making decision, and will cause suffering on the people" (Prov 31:4-5).

My friends, Paul said in Galatians 4:16 "Am I therefore become your enemy, because I tell you the truth?" I also want to say as the apostle Paul said, "Am I therefore become your enemy, because I tell you the truth"?

www.ingramcontent.com/pod-product-compliance
Lightning Source LLC
Chambersburg PA
CBHW051900090426
42811CB00003B/407